Cambridge Little Steps 3

Activity Book

Gabriela Zapiain

CAMBRIDGE
UNIVERSITY PRESS

Cambridge Little Steps 3

① What do we do at school?

👆 Point. 💬 Say. ✏️ Draw

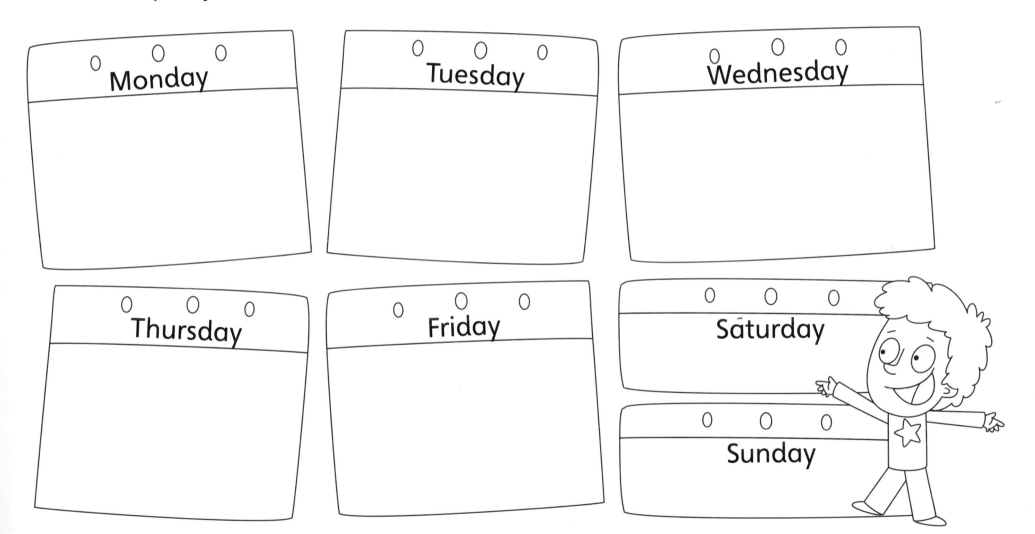

Monday	Tuesday	Wednesday
Thursday	Friday	Saturday
		Sunday

Key Language: *Monday, Tuesday, Wednesday, Thursday, Friday, Saturday, Sunday.* Children point to, and name, each day of the week. Have a class discussion about what they do in school from Monday to Friday and encourage all children to say what they do each day of the week. Finally, children choose a weekday and draw a picture of one thing that they do at school on that day.

3

🔲 Say. ◯ Circle. ✏ Color.

We Learn at School!

Key Language: *What can you see? Who are the characters? Where does the story take place? What's happening? hat, coat, bee, tree, wing.* Children look at the story scenes. Ask the literacy questions. Then ask: *Can you see a coat? Can you see a hat? Can you see a bee? Can you see wings? Can you see a tree?* Children circle, then color the items in the picture.

🗨 Say. ◯ Circle. ✏ Color.

Key Language: What can you see? Who are the characters? Where does the story take place? What's happening? screen, Thursday, Friday. Children look at the story scenes. Ask the literacy questions. Then ask *Can you see a screen? Can you see Thursday? Can you see Friday?* Help them to understand the days of the week on the calendars. Children circle and then color the items in the picture. Finally, children retell the story in their own words. Provide language as needed.

 **Point.** **Say.** **Trace.**

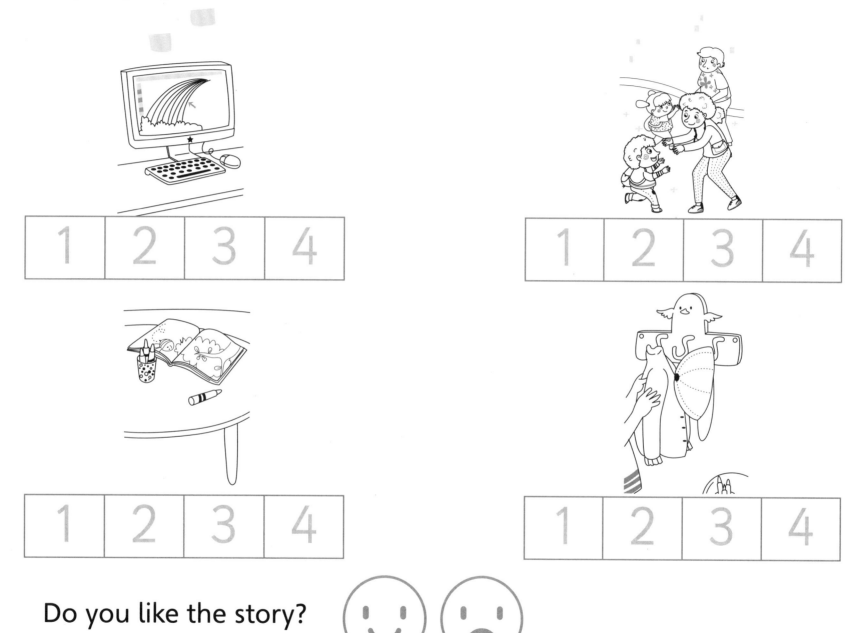

| 1 | 2 | 3 | 4 |

| 1 | 2 | 3 | 4 |

| 1 | 2 | 3 | 4 |

| 1 | 2 | 3 | 4 |

Do you like the story?

Key Language: *Can you remember? What happened first / next / at the end?* Retell the story together as much as possible. Children then look at the scenes. Ask: *Can you remember? What happened first?* Children point to the correct scene (coat and hat). Continue, asking: *What happened next?* with the second and third scenes and: *What happened at the end?* for the final scene. Repeat, this time children tracing or circling the numbers to indicate the correct story order. Finally, ask: *Do you like the story? (Yes. / No.)* Children color the happy face or the sad face.

 Look. 💬 Say. ✏️ Draw

Key Language: *Be kind to others, How can we be kind?* Children look at the picture. Ask children what they think the girl standing up might be saying. Do they think she is complimenting the girl's painting? Discuss what it means to be kind. Ask: *How can we be kind? (helping, sharing, complimenting others, telling them they are good at something).* Invite children to share experiences of when they were complimented and how they felt. Finally, children draw a picture of a situation at school that shows kindness.

7

 Say. Color. Trace.

1. Art

2. Physical Education

3. Reading

Key Language: *Science, Art, Math, Writing, Reading, Physical Education.* Point to each picture and elicit the subject name and have all children repeat. Then ask children to listen carefully and instruct them to color one element from each subject, e.g., the soccer ball, the painting, the books. Say, e.g., *Color the painting red!* Optional: Children trace the words as they repeat them aloud. Then write *Science, Math* and *Writing* on the board and draw simple pictures to illustrate them. Have children identify the subjects.

 **Look.** ✏️ **Draw.** 💬 **Say.**

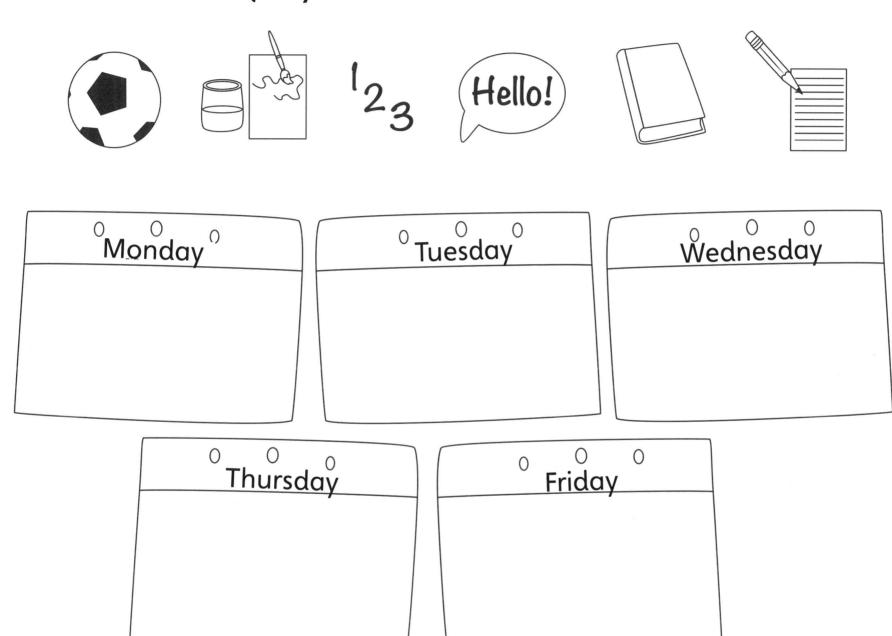

Key Language: *What day is today? (Monday.) What do we have on (Mondays)? We have (Art).* Point to each icon, name the subject and have children repeat. Then ask: *What do we have on Mondays?* Elicit some possible answers, encouraging children to say: *We have (Art). We have (Reading).* Then point to each day of the week, say the word and have children repeat. Children draw at least one of the icons for each day. Finally, children share one of their drawings, saying, e.g., *On Tuesdays, we have Math.*

9

✎ Paint. 💬 Say. ⊙ Trace.

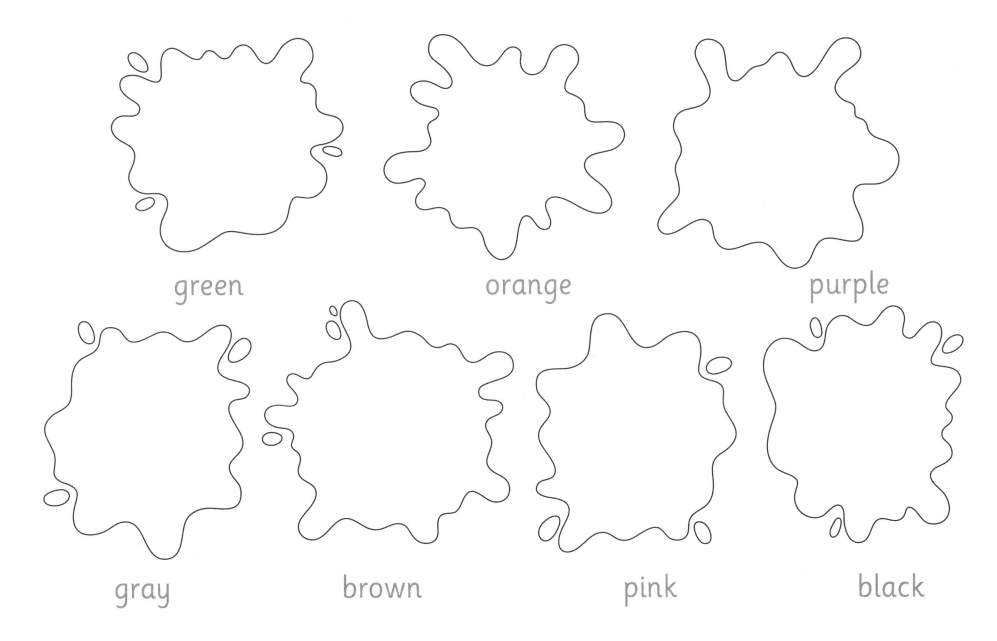

green orange purple

gray brown pink black

Key Language: *green, orange, purple, pink, black, gray, brown, What color is it? It's (red). This is (red).* Point to each color word and read together, children repeating the words aloud. Distribute watercolor paints. Children find the correct color and paint the splotches above the corresponding words. Finally, they present their work, saying: *This is (green). This is (pink).* etc. Optional: Children trace the words.

Match. Color. Trace.

- use a computer

- play music

- speak English

- paint with watercolors

- read books

- play in the playground

Key Language: *use a computer, play music, speak English, paint with watercolors, read books, play in the playground.* Point to and say each vocabulary item and ask children to repeat after you. Then children draw lines to match the words to the corresponding pictures. Finally, they listen carefully and color a key element from each picture. Say, e.g., *Color the computer purple!* Optional: Children trace the words.

👁 Look. 💬 Say. ✏️ Draw.

Key Language: *What does Leo / Mia do at school? S/he plays music / uses a computer / speaks English / paints with watercolors / reads books / plays in the playground.* Point to the first sentence and ask: *What does Leo do at school?* Point to each picture and read the sentence together, e.g., *Leo uses a computer and plays music at school.* Repeat with Mia. Then children draw a friend and two different activities the friend does at school. Ask volunteers to share their drawings and say what their friend does at school.

➡➡ Follow. 🗨 Say. ✏ Draw.

Key Language: *What does s/he need? S/he needs (a chair / paint / a ball).* Point to the first picture and ask: *What does Mia need?* Point to the three options on the right side of the page and ask children: *A chair? Paint? A ball?* Elicit answers. Children follow the maze with their finger and say: *She needs a chair.* Repeat with the remaining pictures. Children then draw the correct paths through the maze using different colored crayons or pencils for each situation.

13

✏ **Draw.** ✏ **Color.** 🔲 **Say.**

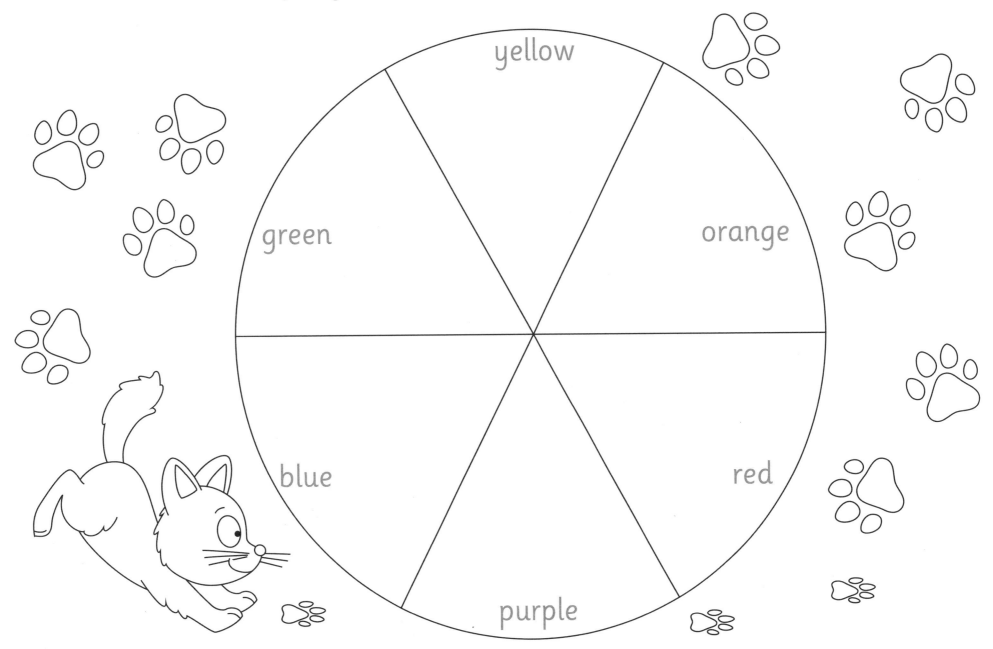

Key Language: *color wheel, primary colors (red, yellow, blue), secondary colors (orange, green, purple).* Point to the color wheel and ask children: *What are the primary colors?* and then point and read the words together. Repeat for secondary colors. Then ask children to name items that are each color, e.g., *What is yellow? (Sun, banana, chick...) What is green? (Leaves, lizard, grapes ...).* Children then draw and color an item of their choice in each section. Finally, they present one of their drawings, saying: *This is a (carrot). It's (orange). It's a (secondary) color.*

2³₁ Count. ✏ Color. ⃝ Trace.

Key Language: *How many (balls) can you see? Let's count: one, two, three ... nineteen, twenty.* Point to the scene and say: *How many balls can you see? Let's count!* Children look at the scene and count the soccer balls. Say: *Twenty! Twenty balls.* Children color the 20 balls and count again. Optional: Children trace the number 20.

15

 **Say.** ✏️ **Draw.**

What do we do at school?

Draw four new words you learned.

Draw a picture of your favorite part of the unit.

How did you do?

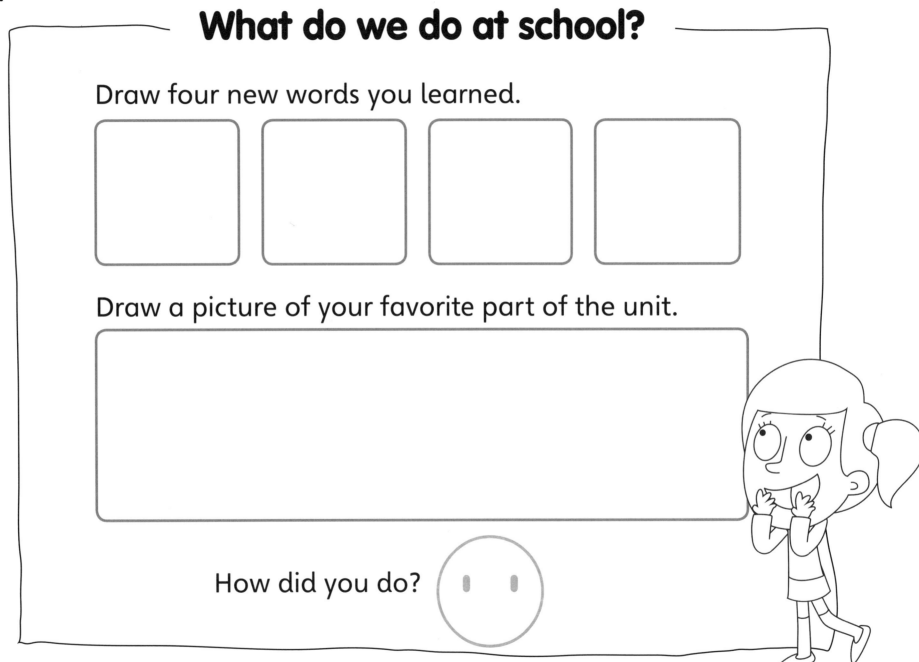

Key Language: *Monday, Tuesday, Wednesday, Thursday, Friday, Saturday, Sunday, What day is today? Science, Art, Math, Writing, Reading, Physical Education, My favorite subject is (Art), We have (Math) on Tuesdays, use a computer, play music, speak English, paint with watercolors, read books, play in the playground, What does s/he do at school? S/he (plays music).* Ask the Big Question: *What do we do at school?* Children look back through the unit to recall what they have learned. Then read the task together and children choose four new things from the unit to draw. Continue with the second task. Finally, guide children to read the last question and have them give themselves a "grade" by drawing a happy or a sad face.

(2) How can we show our feelings?

➡➡ **Follow.** ✏️ **Draw.** ⭕ **Trace.**

scared

excited

silly

bored

shy

surprised

Key Language: *scared, excited, surprised, bored, shy, silly.* Point to the word *scared*, and read together, children repeating aloud. Then demonstrate how to follow the most obvious path by finger tracing to one of the faces. Children repeat the word one more time, then draw a scared expression on the face. Provide help as needed. Repeat with the remaining five words. Optional: Children trace the words.

■ Say. ○ Circle. ✎ Color.

Maddy Goes to a Party

Key Language: *What can you see? Who are the characters? Where does the story take place? What's happening? bake, cake, wait, bored.* Children look at the story scenes. Ask the literacy questions. Then ask: *Can you see a cake? Can you see someone baking a cake? Can you see someone waiting? Can you see someone who is bored?* Children circle and then color the items in the picture.

🗨 Say. ○ Circle. 🖊 Color.

Key Language: *What can you see? Who are the characters? Where does the story take place? What's happening? excited, surprised, happy.* Children look at the story scenes.
Ask the literacy questions. Then ask: *Can you see someone who is excited? Can you see someone who is surprised? Can you see someone who is happy?* Children circle and then
color the items in the picture. Then they retell the story in their own words. Provide language as needed.

 Say. Draw. Color.

Character

Setting

Do you like the story?

Key Language: *Can you remember? Who are the characters? Where does the story take place?* Ask the first two literacy questions, and encourage all answers. They name the characters (Maddy, Uncle Albert, Sophie, Dad), choose their favorite one and draw him / her in the corresponding frame. Then ask: *Where does the story take place?* Children name the places where the story takes place (Maddy's house, outside on the road, Sophie's house) and draw one place in the corresponding frame. Finally, children present their drawings saying, e.g., *This character is Maddy. This setting is Maddy's house.* Finally, ask: *Do you like the story? (Yes. / No.)* Children color the happy face or the sad face.

👁 Look. 💬 Say. ✏️ Draw.

Key Language: *How does s/he feel? S/he feels (sad / scared / bored / shy). Talk about your feelings.* Point to the first picture and ask: *What happened?* Discuss together. Then ask: *How does he feel?* Next, ask children what they think he should do and lead them to the idea that he should talk about his feelings and that it will make him feel better. Finally, children draw the boy talking to someone, making sure the drawing shows how his feeling has changed (he should look happier). Continue in the same way with the second picture.

21

🗨 Say. ✏ Color. ✏ Write.

1. scream

2. shout hooray

3. jump up and down

4. yawn

5. cry

6. laugh

Hooray!

Key Language: *scream, jump up and down, shout hooray, yawn, cry, laugh.* Point to each picture and have children name the action. Repeat several times. Then children color the picture. Optional: Point to the first word and say: *One. scream.* Children repeat and trace the word. Say it again and have children find the picture showing scream and write number 1 in the box. Provide help as needed.

 Say. Match. Color.

1 When I'm    I 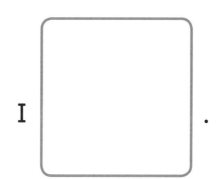 .

2 When I'm    I  .

3 When I'm    I  .

Key Language: *What do you do when you're (bored)? When I'm (bored), I (yawn).* Point to the first part of the first sentence and read together: *When I'm sad, ...* Elicit from children what they do when they're sad: *I cry.* Encourage children to draw a face of someone crying. Continue in the same way with numbers 2 and 3. Finally, encourage children to read the sentences aloud.

👁 Look. 💬 Say. ✏️ Draw.

Key Language: *pattern, What comes next?* Children look at each pattern. They say the feelings aloud and draw the feeling that completes the pattern. Help them to guess the pattern by saying, for example: *Surprised, sad, happy, surprised, sad .... happy!*

2₃¹ Count. ✍ Write. ⭕ Trace.

candy   cake   candle   balloon   present   party hat

Key Language: *candy, cake, candle, balloon, present, party hat.* Children point to and name each party item across the top of the page. Go back to the first item and ask: *How many candies?* Then point to the larger picture and ask children to count how many candies they can find. Children answer, e.g., *Eight! Eight candies.* Optional: Children write the number in the box below each item and trace the words.

👁 Look. 💬 Say. ⭕ Circle.

Key Language: *Can you find the differences? What's different? How many ...?* Children look at the scenes. Ask: *What's different? Can you find the differences?* Children then find and circle the differences in picture 2. If needed, guide children to notice the differences. Say: *Point to the cake in picture one. How many candles are there? (There are five candles.) Now point to the cake in picture two. How many candles are there? (There are six candles.) Let's circle the difference!* Continue in the same manner with the party hat, balloons, and presents.

 Say. 🖊 Draw. 🖊 Color.

Key Language: *How old are you? I'm (five) years old.* Ask children: *How old are you?* and allow several to answer, encouraging the language *I'm ... years old.* Then point to the birthday cake and say: *How many candles?* Children draw a picture of themselves in party clothes, for example, with a party hat and balloons, and draw the correct number of candles on the cake. Then they color their pictures. Finally, they present their pictures, saying: *I'm (six) years old.*

27

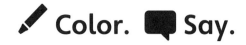 Color. Say.

Key Language: *decorate, Color the (party hat). Decorate the (present).* Prepare and distribute as many arts and crafts resources as you can: watercolor paints, crayons, markers, glitter, small pieces of tissue paper, glue, stickers, etc. Children color and decorate the party hat and present as creatively as they like. Finally, they present their pictures using as much language as they can, e.g., *My party hat is purple and pink. It has stars. My present is green and yellow. It's beautiful.*

2$\frac{1}{3}$ Count. ✏ Color. ✏ Draw.

10   20   30

Key Language: *How many (balloons) can you see? Let's count: one, two, three … twenty … thirty. Sets of ten. Three sets of ten.* Point to the first group of balloons and ask: *How many balloons can you see?* Children count and answer, then color all of the ten balloons in the first group the same color. Continue with the next group. Say: *Let's count by tens!* Point to the number 20 and count: *10, 20.* Children color the second set of balloons in a different color. Then point to number 30 and ask children how many balloons need to go in the last frame. Elicit the number *(10).* Children draw and color ten balloons in a color different to the two colors previously used. Finally, they count by tens to 30.

 Say. ✏ Draw.

How can we show our feelings?

Draw four new feelings you learned.

Draw a picture of your favorite part of the unit.

How did you do?

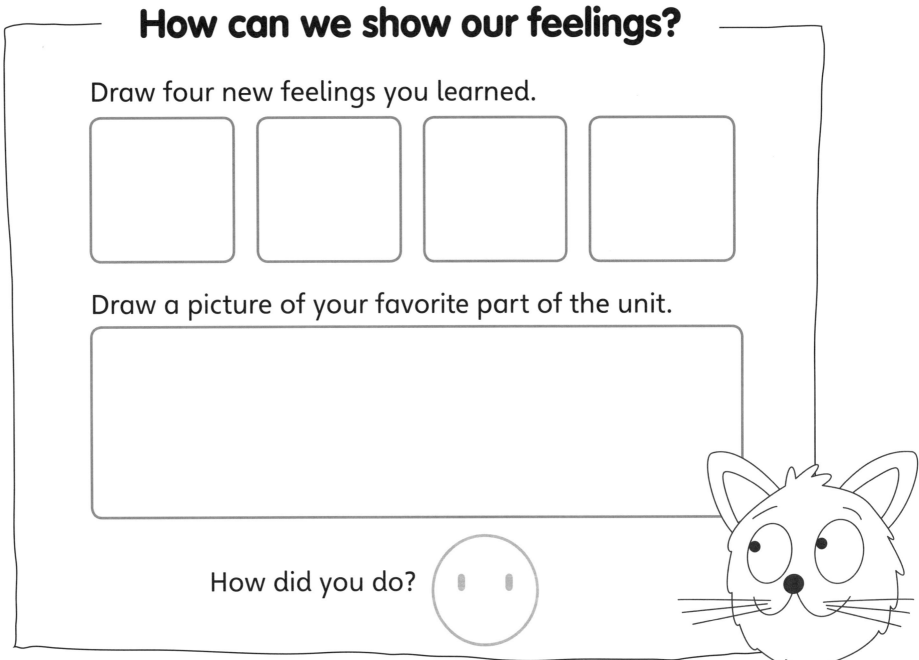

Key Language: *scared, excited, surprised, bored, shy, silly, scream, jump up and down, shout hooray, yawn, cry, laugh, When I'm (bored), I yawn, candy, cake, candle, balloon, present, party hat, birthday party, How old are you? I'm (five) years old.* Ask the Big Question: *How can we show our feelings?* Children look back through the unit to recall what they have learned. Then guide children to read the first two tasks. Read the first, and then the second one together. Children draw their responses. Finally, guide children to read the last question and have them give themselves a "grade" by drawing a happy or a sad face.

3 **How are we the same or different?**

🔲 **Say.** 📘 **Match.** ⭕ **Trace.**

child

men

woman

women

man

children

Key Language: *child, children, woman, women, man, men.* Children look at each picture in the left-hand column and say the vocabulary word. Then they point to, the corresponding picture in the right-hand column and say the plural form of the word. They draw a line to match the singular form to the plural form. Optional: Children trace the words.

■ Say. ○ Circle. ✎ Color.

The Kindergarten Photograph

Key Language: *What can you see? Who are the characters? What's happening? How do the characters feel? tie, glasses.* Children look at the story scenes. Ask the literacy questions. Then ask: *Can you see a tie? Can you see glasses? Can you see someone who is sad?* Children circle, then color the items in the picture.

🗨 Say. ⭕ Circle. ✏ Color.

Key Language: *What can you see? Who are the characters? What's happening? How do the characters feel? line up, glasses.* Children look at the story scenes. Ask the literacy questions. Then ask: *Can you see children lining up? Can you see someone with glasses? Can you see someone who can't walk very well? Can you see someone with curly hair? Can you see someone with straight hair?* Children circle and then color the items in the picture. Finally, they retell the story in their own words. Provide language as needed.

 **Say.** **Draw.**

Main Character

Setting

Do you like the story? 😊 ☹️

Key Language: *Can you remember? Who are the characters? Who is the main character? Where does the story take place*? Explain that the main character is the most important character in a story. Ask: *Who is the main character in this story? (Joana).* Children draw Joana. Ask: *Where does the story take place? (At Joana's house and at school).* Children draw a house and a school inside the Setting frame. Then guide children to say: *Joana is the main character in the story. The story takes place at her house and at her school.* Finally, ask: *Do you like the story? (Yes. / No.)* Children color the happy face or the sad face.

 **Look.** **Say.** **Draw.**

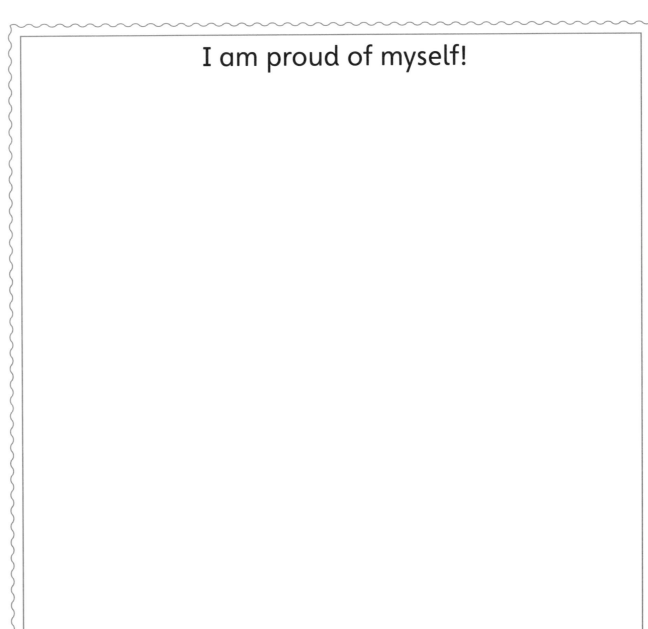

I am proud of myself!

Key Language: *Be proud of yourself. I'm proud of myself. Everyone is different. I'm different.* Say: *Look at Joana. What's missing? (Her glasses.)* Children draw Joana's glasses.
Remind children: *Everyone is different!* and that it's important to respect those differences. Have children think about how they are different. Then they think of one thing about themselves that they feel proud of and draw a picture showing this. Encourage children to share their drawings with the class and say what they feel proud of, e.g., *I'm proud of my hair!*

35

Say. Circle. Trace.

t a l l

s h o r t

a u n t

u n c l e

t h i n

c o u s i n

Key Language: *tall, short, thin, uncle, aunt, cousin.* Children look at the first picture in the left-hand column and say the vocabulary word. Repeat with the remaining pictures and words. Then point to the aunt, uncle and cousin and ask children: *Do you have (an aunt / an uncle / a cousin)?* Children circle those family members they have. Optional: children follow the lines and trace the letters.

 Draw. 💬 Say.

Key Language: *He's a man / boy, She's a woman / girl. S/he's (tall / short / thin).* Children draw an aunt, uncle, or cousin. Then they present their drawings to the class and describe the family member, e.g., *This is my cousin. She's a child. She's a girl. She's short.* Encourage children to use prior knowledge to find other words to describe their family members, for example: *She has long brown hair and green eyes. She's young.*

👁 **Look.** 💬 **Say.** ✏ **Color.**

the tallest

the shortest

Key Language: *short, shorter, the shortest, tall, taller, the tallest. Who is the shortest / tallest?* Children look at the three children in the top row. Ask: *Who is the tallest?* Children point and then say: *This child is the tallest.* Finally, they color the tallest girl. Repeat with the children in the bottom row, asking: *Who is the shortest?*

 **Say.** **Draw.** **Trace.**

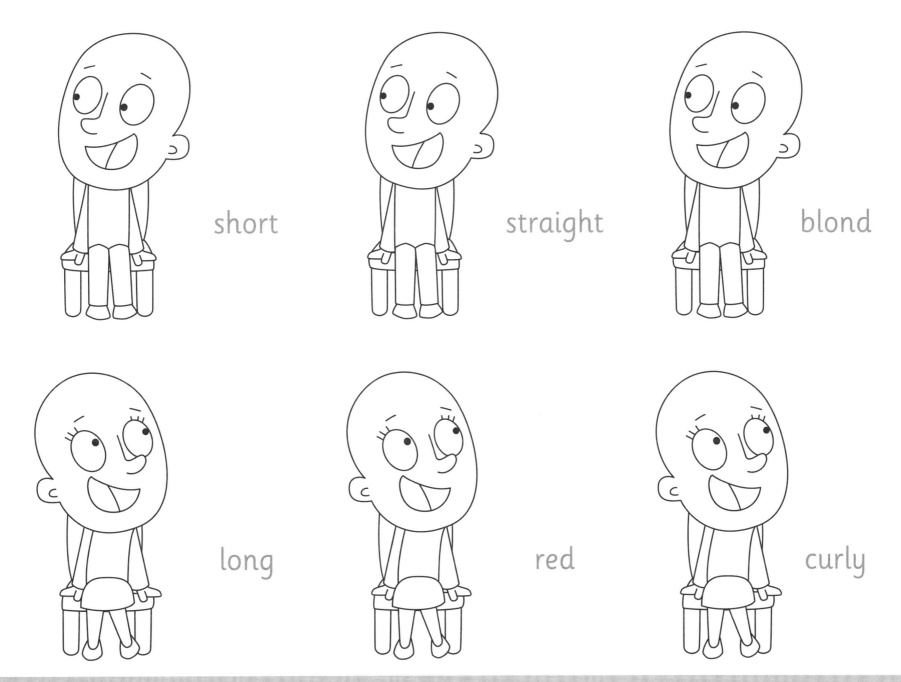

short

straight

blond

long

red

curly

Key Language: *blond, red, long, short, curly, straight.* Point to the first picture of a child and read the word aloud. Children repeat. Then they draw and color the corresponding hair on the picture. Repeat with the remaining words. Optional: Children trace the words.

 **Draw.** **Say.**

My Friend

Key Language: *What does s/he look like? S/he is (short / tall / thin). S/he has (short / long / curly / straight / blond / red / brown / black) hair.* Ask children to think about their friends, at school or at home. Ask: *What does she or he look like?* Children draw one of their friends and describe him or her, e.g., *This is my friend. She has long red hair. She has green eyes. She has glasses.* Children may choose to draw more than one friend if they like or if they finish early.

 Talk. Draw. Say.

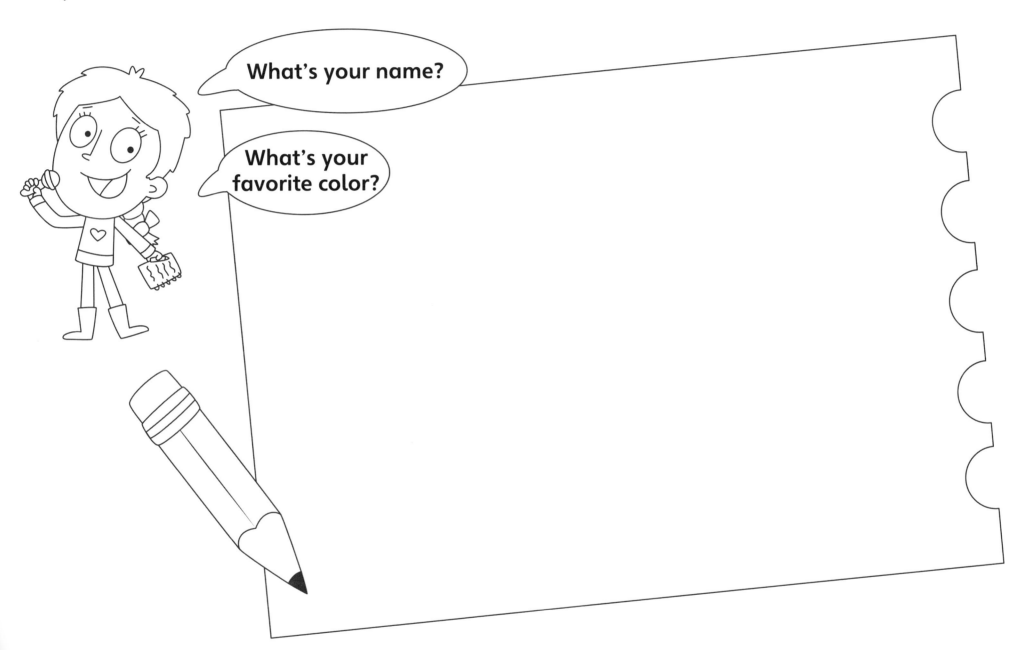

What's your name?

What's your favorite color?

Key Language: *What's your name? My name is ... Her / His name is .... What's your favorite color? My favorite color is ... Her / His favorite color is ...* Select a confident child and ask: *What's your name?* and then: *What's your favorite color?* Once they have responded, draw a simple picture of that child wearing clothes in their favorite color. Arrange children in pairs. They ask one another the two questions and then draw a picture of their partner wearing their favorite colors. Finally, children present their drawings and say: *His/Her name is ... His/Her favorite color is ...*

 Talk. Paint. Say.

My Grandparent

Key Language: *Who's this? This is my grandmother / grandfather). His/Her name is … S/he has (short, gray) hair. S/he has glasses. S/he can't (hear) very well.* Ask children to think about their grandparents. Ask: *What do they look like?* Then ask: *How are they different from parents or children?* Guide children to the ideas that *they are older, they (sometimes) have gray hair, they (sometimes) wear glasses, they (sometimes) can't see or hear or walk very well.* Children choose one grandparent and paint a picture. Make sure you provide gray and white paint. Finally, they present their paintings and describe their grandparent.

2⅓ Count. ○ Circle.

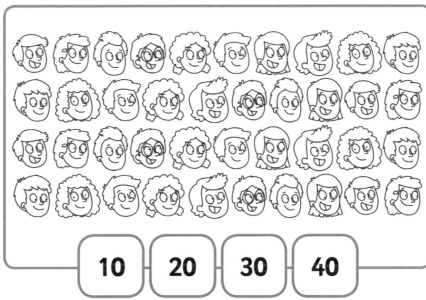

Key Language: *How many (children) can you see? Let's count: one, two, three … twenty. Let's count in tens: twenty, thirty, forty, sets of ten, four sets of ten.* Point to the first group of people and ask: *How many grandparents can you see?* Children count and answer. Then point to the numbers and say them aloud as children repeat: *ten, twenty, thirty, forty.* Children circle the correct number. Then point to the top row of grandparents again and say: *How many? Let's count by tens,* and guide them to notice each row has 10. Count: *ten, twenty.* Continue to the second and third groups of people and count them in tens, children circling the correct numbers.

43

 Say. 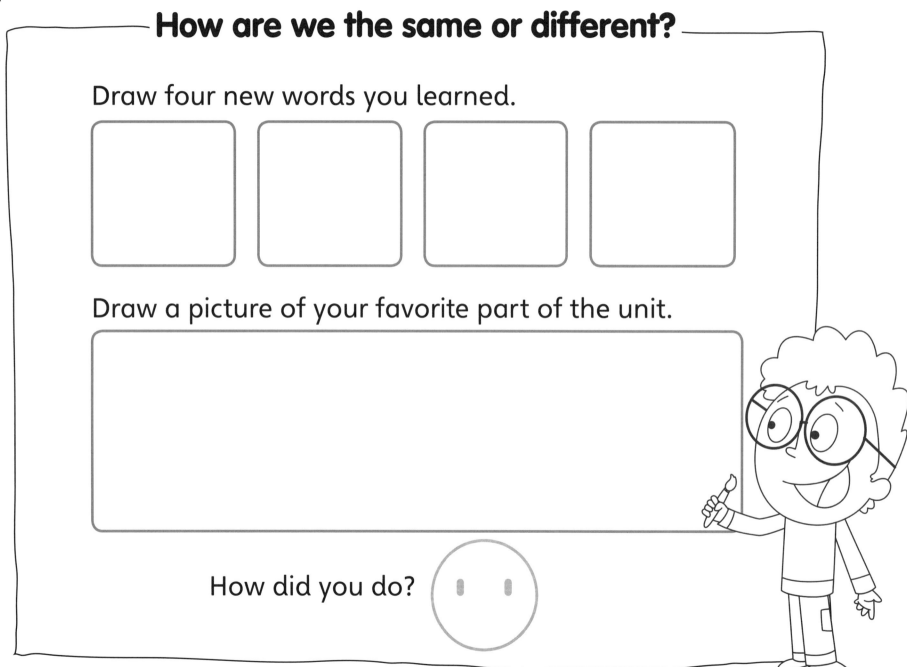 Draw.

How are we the same or different?

Draw four new words you learned.

Draw a picture of your favorite part of the unit.

How did you do?

Key Language: *child, children, woman, women, man, men, aunt, uncle, cousin, tall, short, thin, What does s/he look like? She's a (woman). She's (tall and thin). She has (long) (curly) hair. S/he has (short) (red) hair, What's his / her name? Her / His name is ...* Ask the Big Question: *How are we the same or different?* Children look back through the unit to recall what they have learned. Then guide children to read the first two tasks. Read the first, and then the second one together. Children draw their responses. Finally, guide children to read the last question and have them give themselves a "grade" by drawing a happy or a sad face.

 **What is a wild animal?**

🗨 **Say.** ✏ **Color.** ⬡ **Trace.**

monkey

lion

giraffe

tiger

bear

elephant

Key Language: *monkey, lion, giraffe, tiger, bear, elephant.* Children look at the picture of each animal and say its name. Then they color the animals. Optional: Children say and trace the words while repeating them aloud.

🔲 Say. ◯ Circle. ✏️ Color.

Don't Feed the Wild Animals

Key Language: *What can you see? Who are the characters? What's happening? Where does the story take place? cute, rule.* Children look at the story scenes. Ask the literacy questions. Then ask: *Can you see someone called Sue? Can you see the rules? Can you see a cute animal?* Children circle, then color the items in the picture.

🔲 Say. ⭕ Circle. ✏️ Color.

Key Language: *What can you see? Who are the characters? What's happening? Where does the story take place? elephant, bear.* Children look at the story scenes. Ask the literacy questions. Then ask: *Can you see an elephant? Can you see a bear?* Children circle, then color the items in the picture. Finally, they retell the story in their own words. Provide language as needed.

 **Say.** **Draw.** **Color.**

Characters

Setting

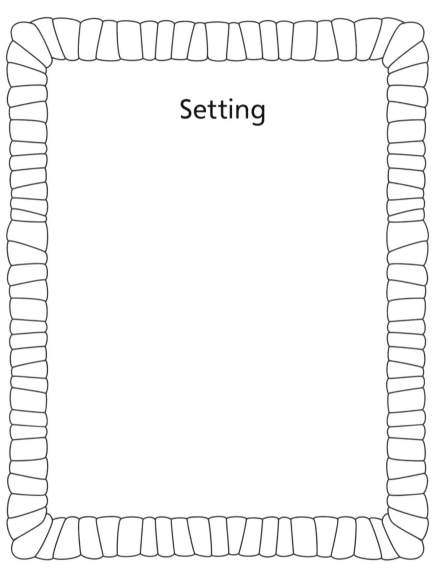

Setting

Do you like the story?

Key Language: *Can you remember? Who are the characters? Where does the story take place?* Ask the first two literacy questions and encourage all answers. Children list the main characters *(Sue, the boy and the bear!)* then draw them. Then ask: *Where does the story take place?* and provide the language *(a safari park or a wildlife park)*. Children draw part of a wildlife park. Finally, ask: *Do you like the story? (Yes. / No.)* Children color the happy face or the sad face.

 **Talk.** **Say.** ✏️ **Draw.**

Protect Wild Animals

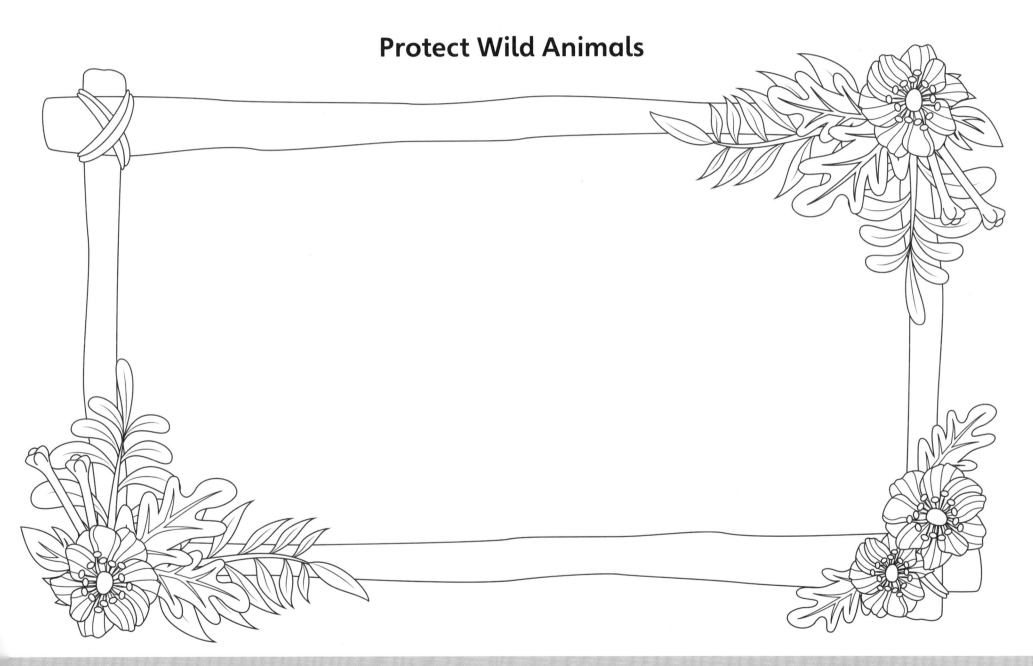

Key Language: *Protect wild animals, Pick up garbage.* Discuss the idea of protecting wild animals and see what the children can recall *(pick up garbage, keep natural areas clean)*. Tell children to imagine they are in a place of natural beauty where wild animals live. They can name the animals and the place (e.g., *the beach, the forest, the park)*. Children draw themselves picking up garbage or cleaning the area, among happy animals.

■ Say. ➡➡ Follow. ◌ Trace.

eagle   kangaroo   toucan   snake   shark   whale

Key Language: *snake, whale, eagle, shark, kangaroo, toucan.* Children point to each animal's head, name the animal and then follow the path to the body of the animal, finger tracing and repeating the word. Then they use a crayon to draw the path, using a different color for each animal. Optional: Children trace the words.

50

 Look. ✏️ Draw. 💬 Say.

Key Language: *Where do (kangaroo)s go? (On land / In the air / In the water).* Look at the scene together and have children point to and name the different places *(land, water, air)*.
Children look at each animal and draw it in the correct place in the scene (in the air, on land, or in the water). Then they say where each animal goes, e.g., *The toucan goes in the air.*

51

$2\frac{1}{3}$ Count. ✏️ Draw. 💬 Say.

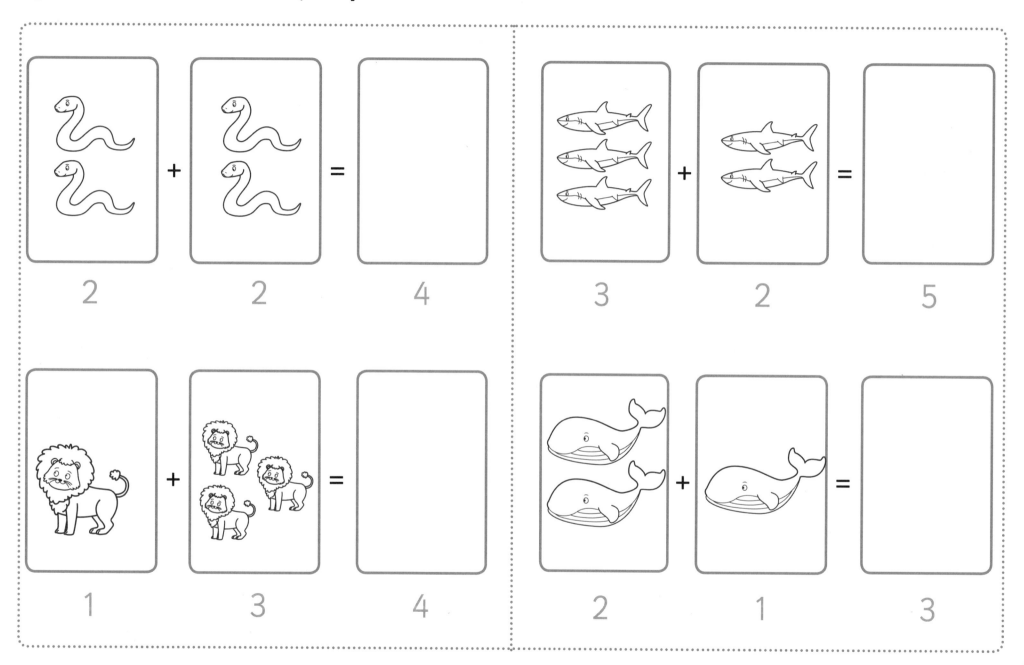

Key Language: *How many (sharks) are there? Let's count. (Three) plus (two) equals (five). There are (five) (sharks).* Look at the first equation with children. Say: *How many snakes are there?* Point to the numbers and say: *Let's count: Two plus two equals...* Encourage children to answer. Once the number is agreed, children draw the total number in the box (*four snakes*). Finally, they say the equation: *Two plus two equals four.* Continue in the same manner with the remaining equations. Optional: Children trace the numbers.

 Look. Say. Trace.

paw

fin

beak

trunk

tail

wing

Key Language: *paw, fin, beak, trunk, tail, wing.* Children look at each picture and name the animal part. Then they trace over the animal part while repeating the word. Optional: Children trace the words.

53

💬 Say. ✏️ Draw. 🖊️ Color.

paw

fin

beak

trunk

tail

wing

Key Language: *What does a (whale) look like? It's (big / small). It's (brown, gray, green...). It has a (long / short) (small / big) neck, fin, tail, beak, trunk, It has (big / small) ears, wings, paws.* Children look at each animal and name the missing part. Then they draw the missing part and color in the animal. Finally, point to each animal and ask: *What does (a tiger) look like? (It's big. It has a long tail. It has big paws. It's orange and black.)*

 **Read.** **Talk.**

Do you like

Do you like  ?

Do you like  ?

Do you like  ?

Key Language: *Do you like (bear)s? Yes, I do. No, I don't. Why / Why not? Because they are (cute / funny/ scary / colorful).* Lead children in reading each question out loud. Demonstrate with a confident child, asking the questions, encouraging answers using the target language, and then asking: *Why or Why not?* Help as necessary providing possible answers. Then arrange children into pairs and have them ask and answer the questions together.

55

 Draw. ✏ Color 🗨 Say.

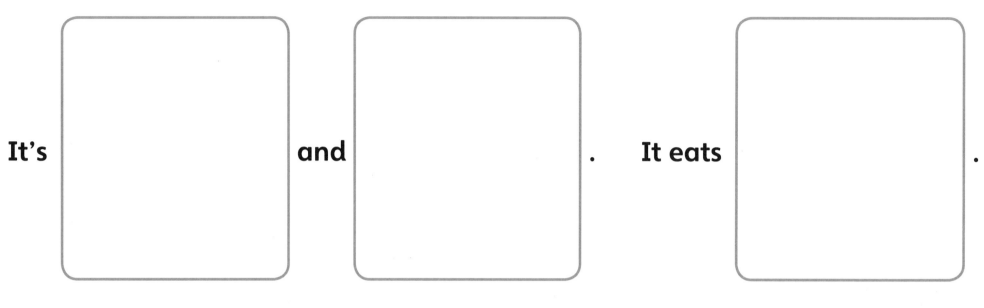

It's [ ] and [ ] . It eats [ ] .

It lives in the [ ] . It is a [ ] .

Key Language: *It's (brown and pink). It eats (fruit). It lives in the (forest). It's a (monkey).* Tell children you are going to describe a wild animal. Children listen carefully and draw or color. Point to the first sentence and read: *It's brown and pink.* Children color in the empty boxes with the correct colors. Continue with: *It eats bananas* and *It lives in the forest* as children draw the pictures in the correct boxes. Finally, say: *It's a ...* and encourage children to guess before saying: *Monkey!* Children draw a monkey in the final box. Then they read the sentences.

²¹₃ Count. ✏ **Draw.** ⬚ **Trace.**

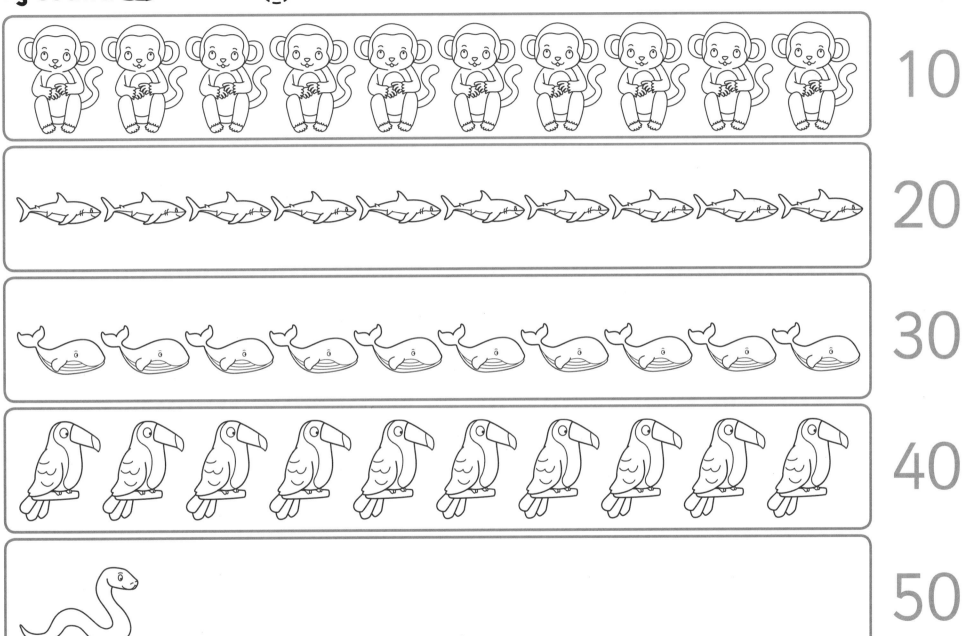

10

20

30

40

50

Key Language: *How many (monkeys) can you see? Let's count by tens: ten, twenty, thirty, forty, fifty. Sets of ten. Five sets of ten.* Point to the first row of animals and ask: *How many monkeys?* Count together, then point to the number 10 and say: *Ten!* Optional: Children trace the number. Then point to the first row again and the next three rows and say: *Let's count in tens: Ten, twenty, thirty, forty.* Point to the bottom row and say: *How many snakes do we need to make 50?* Elicit the answer *(10)* and then children draw nine more snakes to make a total of 50. Finally, count by tens to fifty. Optional: Children trace the numbers as they count.

 Say. ✏️ Draw.

What is a wild animal?

Draw four new animals you learned.

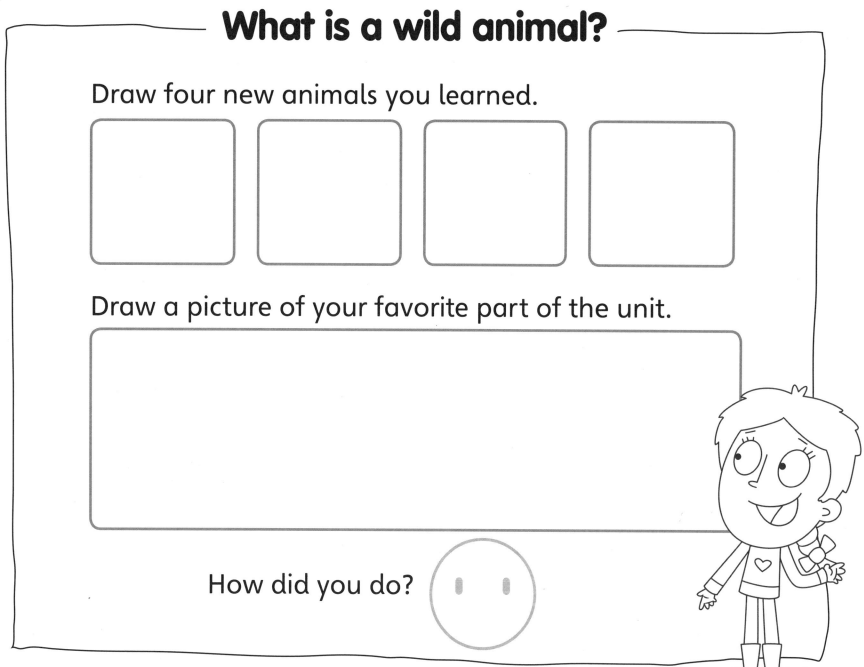

Draw a picture of your favorite part of the unit.

How did you do?

Key Language: *wild animals, monkey, lion, giraffe, tiger, bear, elephant, snake, whale, eagle, shark, kangaroo, toucan, Where do (sharks) go? On land / in the air / in the water, paw, fin, beak, trunk, tail, wing, What does a (giraffe) look like? It's (big / small). It's (brown, gray, green…). It has a (long / short) (small / big) neck, fin, tail, beak, trunk. It has (big / small) ears, wings, paws.* Ask the Big Question: *What is a wild animal?* Children look back through the unit to recall what they have learned. Read the tasks together. Children draw their responses. Finally, guide children to read the last question and have them give themselves a "grade" by drawing a happy or a sad face.

(5) Who works in our community?

✏️ **Color.** 💬 **Say.** ⭕ **Trace.**

① red

② yellow

③ orange

④ black

⑤ blue

cashier

mail carrier   doctor   chef   firefighter   police officer

Key Language: *chef, doctor, cashier, firefighter, mail carrier, police officer.* Children listen as you say the numbers and read the colors. They color in the number circles to make a color key. Then they color the clothes of the corresponding workers. Finally, they point to each and say their name. Optional: Children trace the words as they say them.

59

■ Say. ○ Circle. ✏ Color.

Jewel Goes to School

Key Language: *What can you see? Who are the characters? What's happening? Where does the story take place? snow, bow, mail carrier.* Children look at the story scenes. Ask the literacy questions. Then ask: *Can you see snow? Can you see a bow? Can you see a mail carrier?* Children circle and then color the items in the picture.

■ Say. ○ Circle. ✏ Color.

Key Language: *What can you see? Who are the characters? What's happening? Where does the story take place? teacher, firefighter, froze.* Children look at the story scenes.
Ask the literacy questions. Then ask: *Can you see a teacher? Can you see a firefighter? Can you see a cat that froze?* Children circle and then color the items in the scenes. Finally,
children retell the story in their own words. Provide language as needed.

61

💬 Say. 📖 Match. ✏️ Color.

 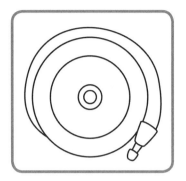  

Do you like the story?

Key Language: *Can you remember? Who does it belong to? I think it belongs to ...* Ask children to look at the top row of objects from the story. Say: *Look. Can you remember? (Yes!)* Then point at the first item, Ruby's book, and ask: *Who does it belong to?* Elicit the answer and guide children to the picture of Ruby in the bottom line. Say: *I think it belongs to the girl/ Ruby.* Ask again and guide children to the answer: *I think it belongs to Ruby.* Children draw a line to match the book and the girl. Continue in the same way with the remaining objects and characters. Finally, ask: *Do you like the story? (Yes. / No.)* Children color the happy face or the sad face.

💬 Talk. ✏️ Draw. 💬 Say.

Key Language: *Respect people in your community. Be polite. Say "thank you".* Ask children: *Who works in our community?* Allow them to list people and provide language as necessary *(teacher, mail carrier, firefighter, doctor, chef, police officer, cashier)*. Discuss how we can show respect for these people *(be polite, say thank you)*. Children choose and draw two people in their community. Finally, they present their drawings using the language, e.g., *This is … S/he is a cashier in my community. I am polite to … I say thank you.*

■ **Say.** ◯ **Circle.** ✎ **Color.**

fire station

hospital

police station

d k a n k e o c p n a a g f i r e s t a t i o n l a t n e w o p o l
r e s t a u r a n t o n k b e l t a g o w m e n t f a n p o w m i s
m e d o g r o c e r y s t o r e a m n t f a t i l h o s p i t a l g
r o a s c a m p o l i c e s t a t i o n h i l q p o s t o f f i c e

grocery store

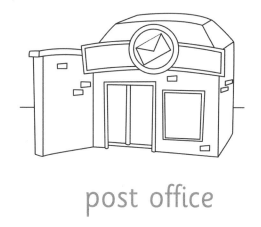

post office

restaurant

Key Language: *fire station, hospital, restaurant, post office, police station, grocery store.* Children look at each picture and word. They say and repeat the word. Optional: Children trace the word as they repeat it. Then they look for the word in the word search puzzle and circle it. Demonstrate first and provide help as needed. Finally, they color the corresponding picture.

👆 Point. ➡️➡️ Follow. 🗨️ Say.

Key Language: Where does a (firefighter) work? S/he works in a (fire station). A firefighter works in a fire station. Children point to the first worker and name the job. Ask: *Where does a (doctor) work?* Children follow the path to find the work place and answer, e.g., *A hospital.* Finally, children say a sentence about where each person works, e.g., *A doctor works in a hospital.*

65

2³⁄₁ Count. 📘 Match. 💬 Say.

6

7

10

5

2

8

Key Language: *How many? (Five) plus (five) equals (ten).* Children look at each pair of dice. Ask: *How many?* They count the dots on each dice and add them together. Then children match the sum to the correct number. Finally, children say the equation aloud, e.g., *Six plus two equals eight.*

Match. Say. Trace.

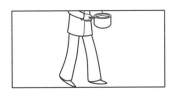
cook food

ring up groceries

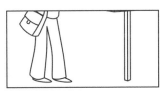
deliver mail

put out fires

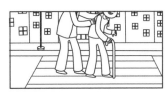
keep people safe

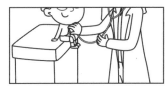
take care of people

Key Language: *put out fires, take care of people, cook food, keep people safe, deliver mail, ring up groceries.* Children draw lines to match the tops and bottoms of the scenes. Then they say the phrases. Optional: children trace the words.

2¹₃ Count. ■ Say. ✏ Color.

Who's he/she?

Where does he/she work?

What does he/she do?

Key Language: *Who's s/he? S/he's a (doctor), Where does s/he work? S/he works in a (hospital), What does s/he do? S/he (takes care of people).* Say a number from one to eighteen. Beginning at *Start*, children count that number of squares. Ask volunteers to say sentences about the picture, e.g., *He is a chef. He works in a restaurant. He cooks food.* Ask questions to prompt, e.g., *Who works here? Who's he? What does she do?* Children color the picture. Continue until all pictures have been colored in.

 Follow. ◯ Trace. ■ Say.

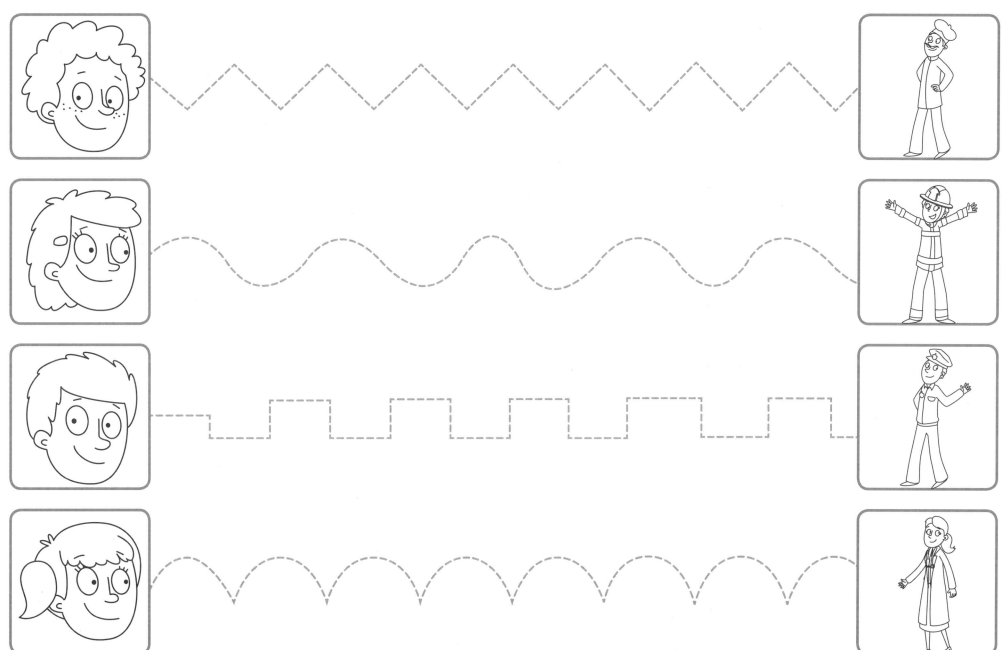

Key Language: *What do you want to be? I want to be a ... What does s/he want to be? S/he wants to be a...* Point to the first child and ask: *What does he want to be?* Children follow the lines to discover what each child wants to be when they grow up. Then they trace the lines. Finally, they answer the question with a sentence, e.g., *He wants to be a chef.*

💬 Talk. 🖍 Glue. ✏ Color.

Key Language: *This is a firefighter. He puts out fires.* Point to the firefighter and ask children to talk about him. Provide question prompts if necessary: *Who is he? What does he do? Where does he work?* Discuss all the different ways he helps people (e.g., *He puts out fires. He helps people in accidents. He helps cats in trees!* Then demonstrate how to cut or tear strips of tissue paper and glue them to the scene to create the flames. Finally, children color the firefighter. If possible, it would be ideal to have a firefighter visit the class or go on a trip to a fire station.

 Count. 🔲 Say. ○ Circle.

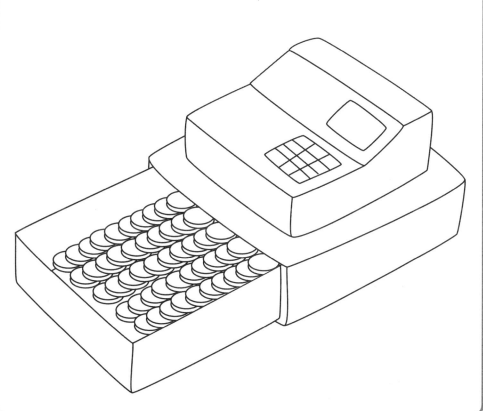

40   50   60   40   50   60

Key Language: *How many (coins / cookies) can you see? Let's count by tens: ten, twenty, thirty, forty, fifty, sixty. Sets of ten. Six sets of ten.* Point to the cash register and ask: *How many coins?* Guide children to notice that they are arranged in sets of tens. Say: *Let's count by tens: ten, twenty, thirty, forty, fifty!* Children circle the correct number below the picture. Repeat for the cookies.

 Say. Draw.

Who works in our community?

Draw four new jobs you learned.

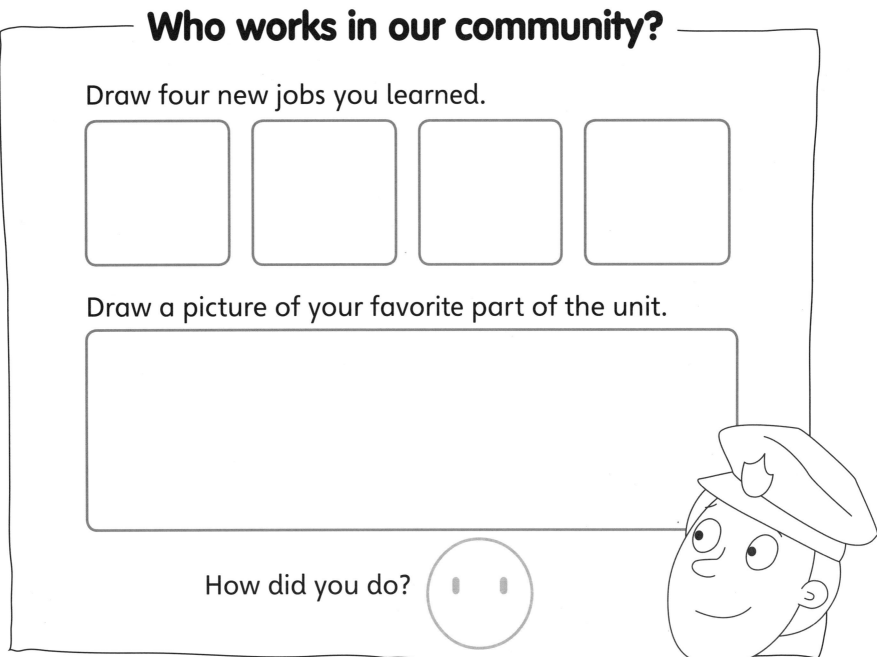

Draw a picture of your favorite part of the unit.

How did you do?

Key Language: *people in our community, firefighter, doctor, chef, police officer, mail carrier, cashier, fire station, hospital, restaurant, police station, post office, grocery store,* *Where does s/he work? A (chef) works in a (restaurant). What do (chefs) do? They (cook food), put out fires, take care of people, keep people safe, deliver mail, ring up groceries.* Ask the Big Question: *Who works in our community?* Children look back through the unit to recall what they have learned. Then guide children to read the first two tasks. Children draw their responses. Finally, guide children to read the last question and have them give themselves a "grade" by drawing a happy or a sad face.

 Why are restaurants special?

🔲 **Say.** ✏️ **Color.** ⭕ **Trace.**

waiter

drink

main dish

side dish

dessert

Key Language: *waiter, menu, drink, main dish, side dish, dessert.* Point to each item and say the word aloud and have children repeat. Finally, children color the items as they repeat the word. Optional: Children trace the words.

■ Say. ○ Circle. ✏ Color.

Uncle Piero's Special Restaurant

Key Language: *What can you see? Who are the characters? What's happening? Where does the story take place? meet, restaurant.* Children look at the story scenes. Ask the literacy questions. Then ask: *Can you see the boys meeting someone? Can you see a restaurant?* Children circle and then color the items in the picture.

🔲 Say. ⭕ Circle. ✏️ Color.

Key Language: *What can you see? Who are the characters? What's happening? Where does the story take place? chef, see, teach, cook, eat.* Children look at the story scenes. Ask the literacy questions. Then ask: *Can you see a chef? Can you see the chef teaching the boys how to cook? Can you see the boys eating?* Children circle and then color the items in the picture.

75

Characters

Setting

Do you like the story?

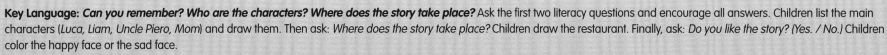

Key Language: *Can you remember? Who are the characters? Where does the story take place?* Ask the first two literacy questions and encourage all answers. Children list the main characters (*Luca, Liam, Uncle Piero, Mom*) and draw them. Then ask: *Where does the story take place?* Children draw the restaurant. Finally, ask: *Do you like the story? (Yes. / No.)* Children color the happy face or the sad face.

 **Talk.** ✏ **Draw.** ◯ **Trace.**

Be polite in restaurants.

Key Language: *Be polite in restaurants.* Point to the boy in the picture and ask: *Where is he? (In a restaurant.)* Read the sentence aloud. Children repeat. Discuss different ways children can be polite in restaurants (say *please* and *thank you* to the waiter, sit quietly, appreciate your food, etc.). Invite children to share their own experiences. Finally children draw themselves in a restaurant being polite. Optional: Children trace the sentence.

77

🗨 Say. ✏ Color. ✎ Write.

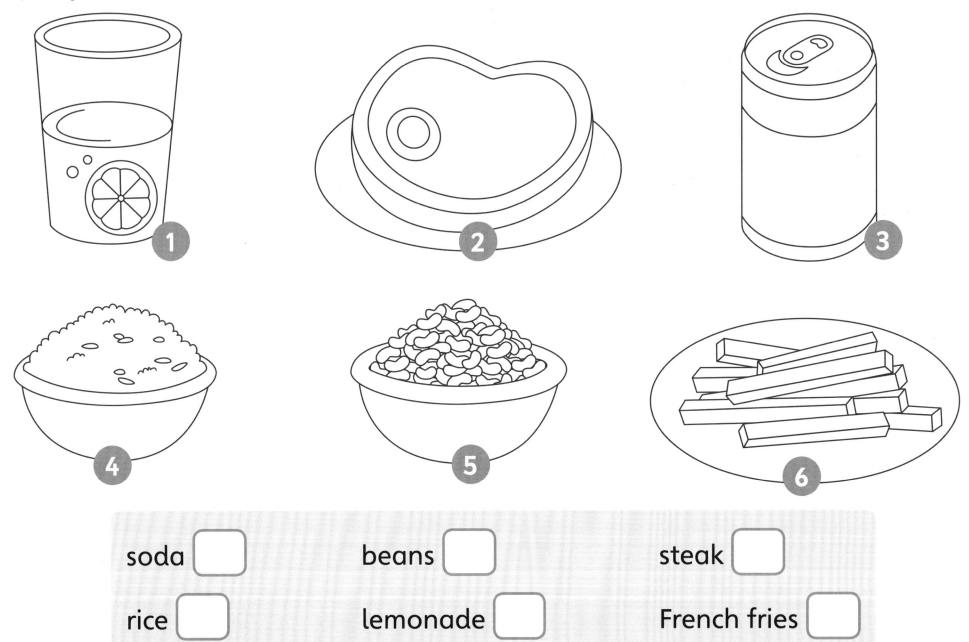

soda ☐

rice ☐

beans ☐

lemonade ☐

steak ☐

French fries ☐

Key Language: *steak, beans, rice, French fries, soda, lemonade.* Children point and say the name of each item aloud. Finally, children color the pictures of the food or drink they like. Optional: They write the number of each item next to the correct word or words.

👁 Look. 💬 Say. ✏ Color.

🙂 She likes lemonade.

🙁 She doesn't like lemonade.

🙂 She likes French fries.

🙁 She doesn't like French fries.

🙂 He likes beans.

🙁 He doesn't like beans.

🙂 He likes steak.

🙁 He doesn't like steak.

Key Language: *Does s/he like (beans)? Yes, she does. No, s/he doesn't. She/He likes soda. She/He doesn't like beans.* Point to the first picture and ask: *Does she like lemonade?* Allow children to look at the picture and decide, then give their answer *(No, she doesn't.)* Rephrase, point to the sentence and sad face and say: *She doesn't like lemonade.* Children repeat and then color the correct face. Continue in the same way with the remaining three pictures.

79

2^1_3 Count. ✏️ Draw. 💬 Say.

Key Language: *How many? Let's count. More than, Less than, (Six) is more than (three). symbol.* Review the signs <, >, and = with children. Use the language *Less than, More than* and *Equal to.* Direct their attention to the first picture. Point and say: *How many? Let's count.* Count the number of dots on the domino together as a class. Then point to the sign. Ask: *What does this symbol mean? (More than!)* Then say: *What is more than 1?* Children can name any number greater than one (up to six). Children draw the corresponding number of dots on the domino. Finally, children say, e.g., *Three is more than one.*

 **Say.** **Color.** **Trace.**

spaghetti

pizza

ice cream

chocolate cake

cheeseburger

vegetables

Key Language: *spaghetti, pizza, ice cream, chocolate cake, vegetables, cheeseburger.* Children point to each food item and say the name, repeating several times. Finally, they color the food they like. Optional: Children trace the word as they repeat it.

▪ Say. ○ Circle. ✎ Color.

Key Language: *What do we need to eat (steak)? We need a fork / knife / spoon and a plate / bowl to eat (steak).* Children look at each food item and name them. Ask: *What do we need to eat spaghetti?* Elicit answers using the language: *We need a fork and a plate to eat spaghetti.* Children circle the fork and plate. Note there are different possible answers and allow children to share how they eat different foods. Continue in the same manner with the remaining food items. Finally, children color each food or drink item and the things they need to eat or drink it.

✏️ Draw. ✏️ Color. 💬 Say.

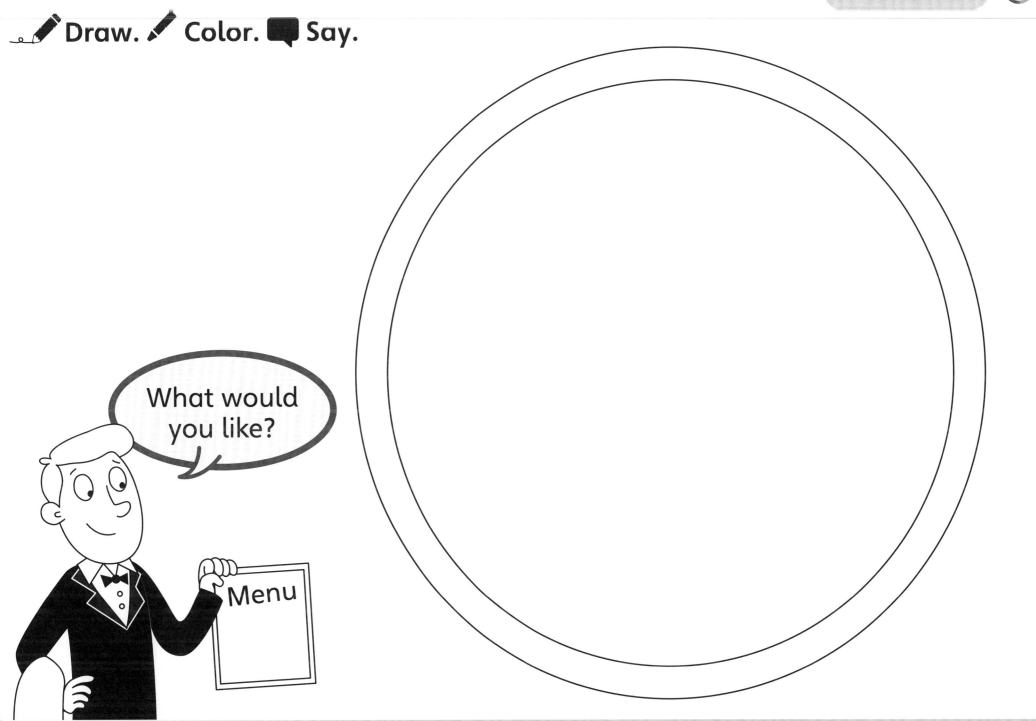

Key Language: *What would you like? I would like (steak) and (vegetables), please.* Guide children to read the question. Then have them draw and color what they would like to eat. Finally, ask individual children to share their pictures with the class and say what they would like to eat, using the language, e.g., *I would like pizza and ice cream, please.*

83

 **Draw.** ✏ **Color.** 🗨 **Say.**

Is it a fruit or a vegetable?

Draw a green vegetable.

Draw a red fruit.

Draw an orange fruit.

Draw an orange vegetable.

Key Language: *Is it a fruit or a vegetable? It's a (carrot). I think it's a fruit / vegetable.* Look at the first box and read the sentence together. Allow children time to think about, draw and color their own idea. Continue with the remaining three boxes. Finally, children present their drawings, using the language, e.g., *It's a (cucumber). I think it's a (vegetable).*

2¹₃ Count. ✏ Write.

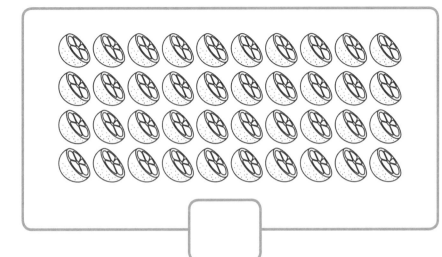

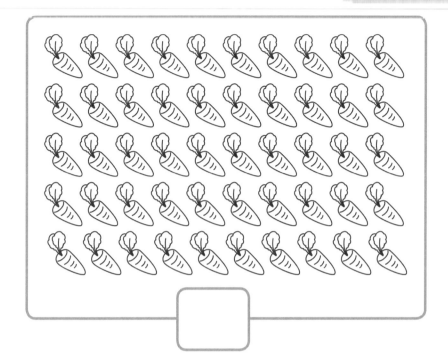

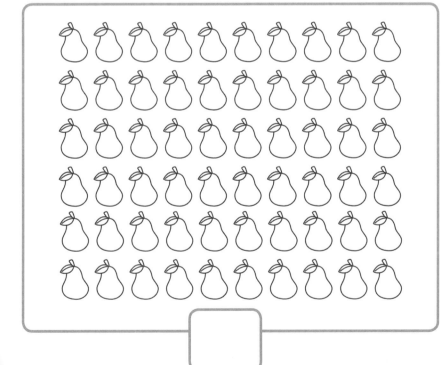

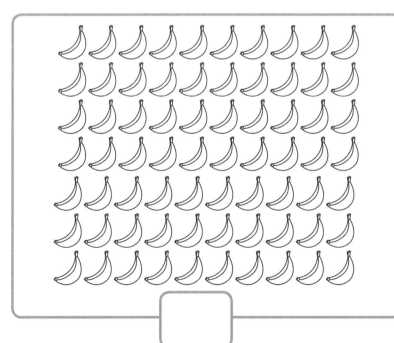

Key Language: *How many fruits / vegetables can you see? Let's count by tens: ten, twenty, thirty, forty, fifty, sixty, seventy. Sets of ten. Seven sets of ten.* Look at the first box and ask children: *How many fruits can you see?* Discuss the easiest way to count (by tens). Say: *Let's count by tens: Ten, twenty, thirty, forty. Forty fruits.* Repeat with the remaining boxes. Optional: Children write the number in the box. Give guidance as necessary or write the number on the board for children to copy.

 Say. Draw.

Why are restaurants special?

Draw four new food items you learned.

Draw a picture of your favorite part of the unit.

How did you do?

Key Language: *waiter, menu, drink, main dish, side dish, dessert, steak, beans, rice, French fries, soda, lemonade, Do you like (beans)? Yes, I do, No, I don't. I like (beans). I don't like (soda). S/he likes (steak). S/he doesn't like (rice), spaghetti, pizza, ice cream, chocolate cake, vegetables, cheeseburger. We need a (spoon / fork / knife) and a (bowl / plate) to eat (spaghetti).* Ask the Big Question: *Why are restaurants special?* Children look back through the unit to recall what they have learned. Read the first two tasks together. Children draw their responses. Finally, guide children to read the last question and have them give themselves a "grade" by drawing a happy or a sad face.

 **7** # What does a routine look like?

🗨 **Say.** ✎ **Write.** ⬭ **Trace.**

do homework

go to school

get up

have breakfast

go home

get dressed

Key Language: *get up, get dressed, have breakfast, go to school, go home, do homework.* Children look at each picture and name the action. Then discuss the order in which children do the actions. Optional: Children number the pictures in the order they do each action during day and trace the words.

■ Say. ○ Circle. ✏ Color.

The Hare and the Tortoise

Key Language: *What can you see? Who are the characters? What's happening? clock, have breakfast.* Children look at the story scenes. Ask the literacy questions. Then ask: *Can you see a clock? Can you see an animal having breakfast?* Children circle and then color the items in the picture.

◼ Say. ◯ Circle. ✏ Color.

Key Language: *What can you see? Who are the characters? What's happening? clock, clothes, cry, tree.* Children look at the story scenes. Ask the literacy questions. Then ask: *Can you see an animal wearing clothes? Can you see an animal crying? Can you see a tree? Can you see an animal sleeping?* Children circle and then color the items in the picture. Finally, children retell the story in their own words. Provide language as needed.

👁 Look. 🗨 Say. 📖 Match.

1 First

2 Next

3 End

Do you like the story? 🙂 🙁

Key Language: *Put the story in order. What happens What happens first / next / at the end?* Say: *Do you remember the story? Let's put the story in order!* Children open their books. Point to the pictures and ask: *Do you remember? What happens first? (Hare gets up and has breakfast. Hare drinks the juice). And what happens next? (Hare has a nap.) And what happens at the end? (Hare cries).* Go back to the first picture and help children find the word *Next,* and match it with the scene. Continue in the same manner with the remaining scenes, encouraging children to use the language.

👁 Look. 💬 Talk. ✏️ Draw.

Key Language: *Follow a routine, What do you do every day?* Children look at the stages in the girl's daily routine. Point to each and ask: *Do you do this every day?* Discuss why it's important to have a routine and to do these things every day. Ask: *What do you do every day?* Children respond. Provide new language as necessary. Finally, children draw pictures of four activities in their daily routine and then present to the class.

 **Say.**  **Match.**  **Write.**

1 dance class

2 soccer practice

3 music lessons

4 swimming lessons

5 play with friends

6 gymnastics

Key Language: *dance class, soccer practice, music lessons, swimming lessons, play with friends, gymnastics.* Point to number 1 and read aloud. Children repeat and then find the corresponding picture. Children draw lines to match the word to the picture and children use different colors for each item so the matching is clearer. Continue in this way for the remaining vocabulary items. Optional: Children trace the word as they say it and write the corresponding number in the box.

✏️ Color. ✏️ Draw. 💬 Say.

music lessons

play with friends

soccer practice

Key Language: *What do you do after school? I have (swimming lessons). I play with friends.* Ask children: *What do you do after school?* Children color the pictures that show activities they do in the afternoon. Then they draw and color themselves doing an activity they regularly do in the afternoon. Finally, children share their drawings and say what they do, e.g., *I have music lessons in the afternoon.*

93

2$\frac{1}{3}$ Count. Match. Write.

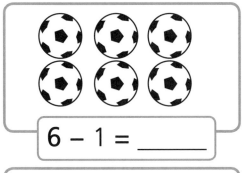

6 – 1 = _____

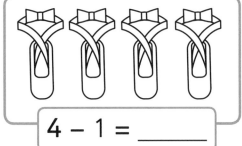

4 – 1 = _____

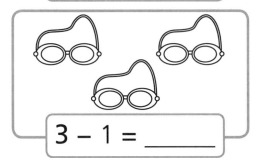

3 – 1 = _____

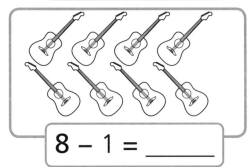

8 – 1 = _____

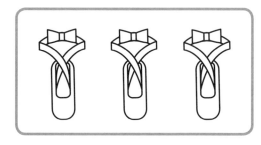

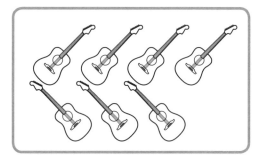

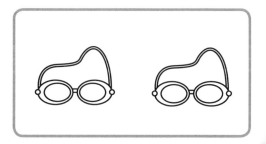

Key Language: *take away one, minus, (Four) minus (one) equals (three).* Read the first equation aloud: *Six minus one equals ...* Guide children to count the soccer balls and cross out the last one. They count the remaining balls to solve the subtraction problem. Finally, they draw a line to the correct picture on the right. Repeat the equation including the answer. *(Six minus one equals five.)* and children repeat. Continue in this manner with the remaining subtraction problems. Optional: Children write the answer.

◯ Trace. 🗨 Say. ✏ Color.

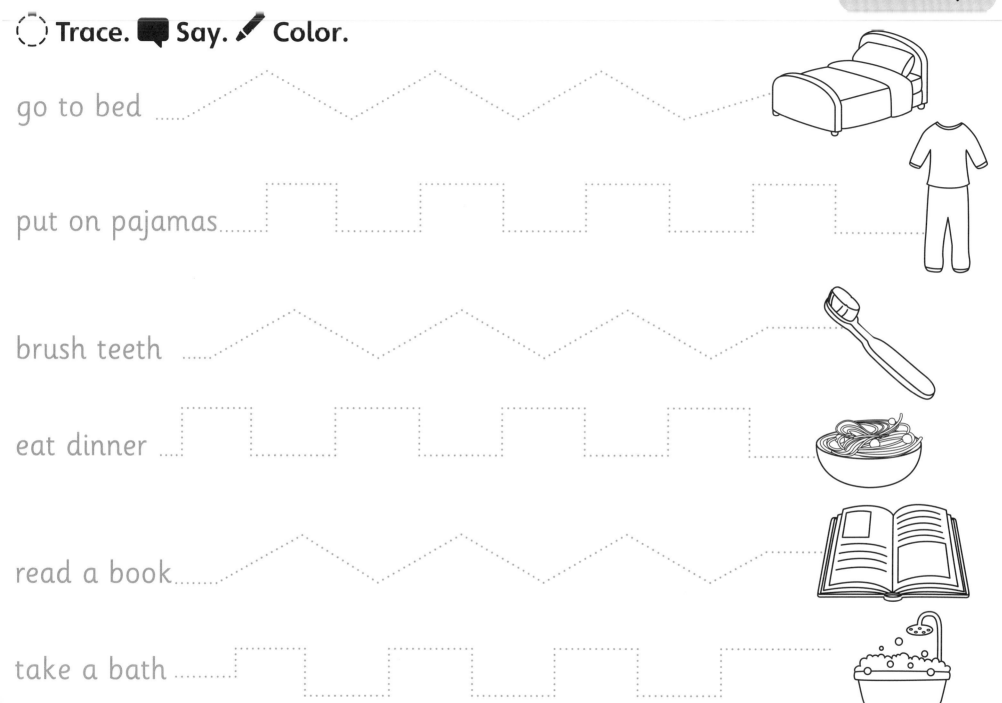

go to bed

put on pajamas

brush teeth

eat dinner

read a book

take a bath

Key Language: *eat dinner, take a bath, brush teeth, put on pajamas, read a book, go to bed.* Ask: *What do you do in the evening?* Point to the first vocabulary item, read it aloud and have children repeat. Then they trace the joining line to the corresponding picture. Finally, they repeat the word and color the picture. Continue in this way with the remaining items. Optional: They trace the word as they say it.

👁 Look. ⭕ Circle. 🗨 Say.

✓✓ = always	✓ = sometimes	✗ = never

1   I   ✓✓ / ✓ / ✗   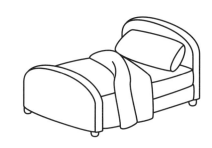   before I      .

2   I   ✓✓ / ✓ / ✗      before I      .

3   I   ✓✓ / ✓ / ✗      before I   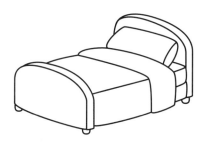   .

Key Language: *What do you do in the evening? always, sometimes, never. I always brush my teeth. I sometimes read a book. I never take a bath in the evening.* Look at the key together and explain the meaning of the three symbols. Then ask children: *What do you do in the evening?* Have children follow along as you read each sentence to them: *I always, sometimes, or never go to bed before I brush my teeth.* Children circle the correct symbol according to their own routines. Finally, invite children to say their sentences for the class.

 Talk. ✏️ Draw. 💬 Say.

Key Language: *I'm bored. What do you want to do? I don't know, Let's (paint / listen to music / play soccer / play a game / eat ice cream / read a book).* Children look at the pictures as you read aloud: *I'm bored! What do you want to do?* Discuss ideas with the class. Finally, children draw their idea and then present to the class, using the llanguage, e.g., *Let's play a game!*

97

👁 Look. 📖 Match. 💬 Say.

It's 6 o'clock.

It's 11 o'clock.

It's 3 o'clock.

Key Language: *What time is it? It's (ten) o'clock, minute hand, hour hand.* Point to the first clock. Ask: *What time is it?* and read the time aloud. Children repeat after you: *It's three o'clock.* Then point to the written times at the bottom of the page and say: *It's three o'clock. Can you find it?* Help children find the correct text. Children draw a line to match the clock and the written time. Continue with the other clocks and times, encouraging children to say the time as they match.

➜➡ Follow. 2¹₃ Count. ◯ Trace.

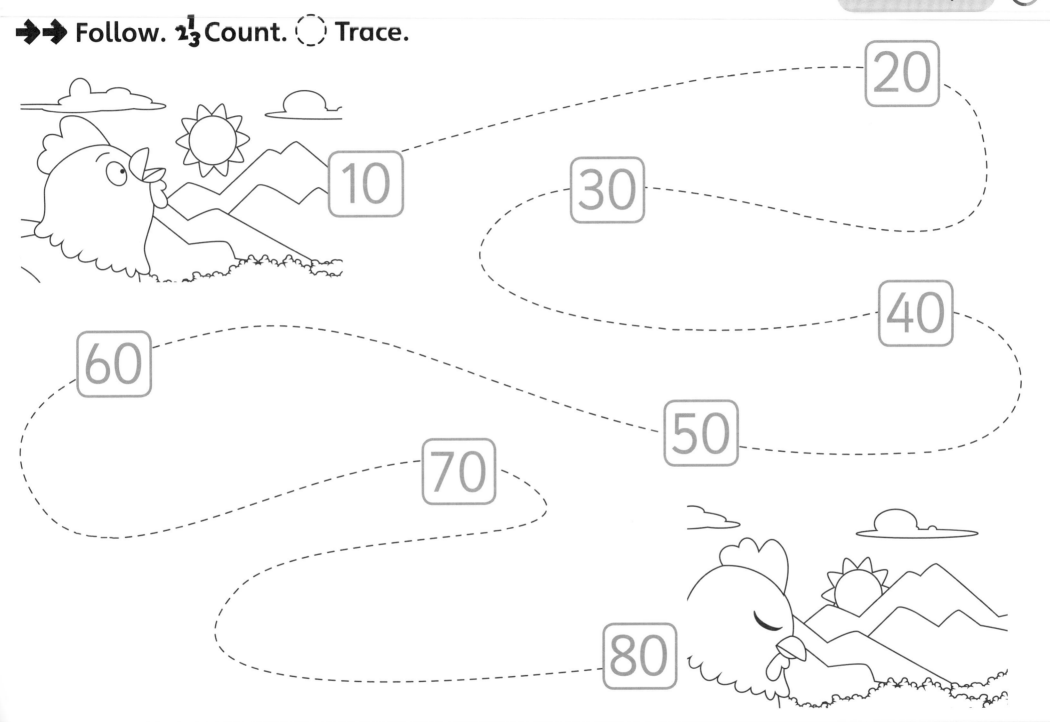

Key Language: *Let's count by tens: ten, twenty, thirty, forty, fifty, sixty, seventy, eighty.* Children follow the path and count by tens as they go. Optional: Children trace the numbers as they follow the path, repeating the words.

99

 Say. ✏️ Draw.

What does a routine look like?

Draw four new words you learned.

Draw a picture of your favorite part of the unit.

How did you do?

Key Language: *get up, get dressed, have breakfast, go to school, go home, do homework, What do you do after school? I have dance class / soccer practice / music lessons / swimming lessons / gymnastics, I play with friends. What do you do in the evening? I have dinner / take a bath / brush teeth / put on pajamas / read a book / go to bed, always, sometimes, never. I (always) (brush my teeth).* Ask the Big Question: *What does a routine look like?* Children look back through the unit to recall what they have learned. Read the tasks together and have children draw their responses. Read the last question and have children give themselves a "grade" by drawing a happy or a sad face.

8 How can we care for the Earth?

Say. **Match.** **Color.**

frog

rock

paper

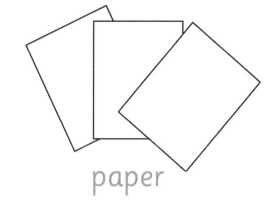

plastic bottle

natural

human-made

Key Language: *natural, human-made, frog, rock, paper, plastic bottle.* Children look at the pictures, say the words, and match the natural items to the tree and the human-made items to the person. Next, they color the natural items green and the human-made items gray. Optional: Children trace the words.

101

 Say. ○ Circle. ✏ Color.

The Yard Guard

Key Language: *What can you see? Who are the characters? What are they doing? Where does the story take place? What's the story about? butterfly, worm, Stevie, plants.*
Children look at the story scenes. Ask the literacy questions. Then ask: *Can you see a boy called Stevie? Can you see a butterfly? Can you see plants? Can you see a worm?* Children circle and then color the items in the picture.

🗨 Say. ○ Circle. ✏ Color.

Key Language: *What can you see? Who are the characters? What are they doing? Where does the story take place? What's the story about? Stevie, squirrel, birds, fly, stand, scatter, seed, smart.* Children look at the story scenes. Ask the literacy questions. Then ask: *Can you see Stevie scattering seeds? Can you see birds flying down? Can you see a squirrel standing? Can you see a smart squirrel?* Children circle and then color the items in the picture. Finally, children retell the story in their own words. Provide language as needed.

103

 Draw. 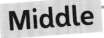 Say. Color.

Beginning

Middle

End

Do you like the story?

Key Language: *What happens in the story? Let's tell the story, the beginning, middle, end.* Remind children of the different parts of a story: *The* beginning *is what happens first. The* middle *is what happens next. The* end *is what happens last.* Children draw what happens in the beginning, the middle, and the end of the story. Invite volunteers to share their drawings and say, e.g., *In the beginning, Stevie waters the plants.* Finally, ask: *Do you like the story? (Yes. / No.)* Children color the happy face or the sad face.

📢 Say. ✏️ Color. 💬 Talk.

Key Language: *save water, don't waste water.* Children look at each scene and decide if the children take are saving or wasting water. Then they color the people who are saving water. Finally, discuss why it's important to save water and what we can do to save water (turn off the faucet, take short showers, use containers instead of running water, etc.).

Say. **Match.** **Color.**

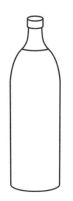

spoon

glass bottle

newspaper

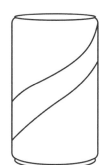

soda can

cardboard box

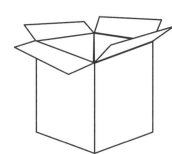

jar

Key Language: *cardboard box, soda can, newspaper, spoon, jar, glass bottle.* Children look at each picture and name the item. Then point to the list of words and read the first one aloud: *spoon.* Children draw lines to match the word to the corresponding picture. Finally, children color the pictures. Optional: Children trace the words as they repeat them.

👁 Look. ✏ Color. 💬 Say.

Four in a Row

Key Language: *What is it? It's a ... Is it natural or human-made? I think it's (natural).* Children look at the objects on the game board. Explain that some are natural and some are human-made. Tell them you are going to play a game where they need to listen and color, and that the objective is to get four colored objects in a row (across or down). Say: *Color something natural!* and children choose one item to color from anywhere in the game. Next say: *Color something human-made* and they do the same. Continue in this way, randomly choosing natural or human-made. When a child has colored four items in a row, they point to each and say *natural* or *human-made*. Play several times.

2 $\frac{1}{3}$ Count. ✏ Draw. 🗨 Say.

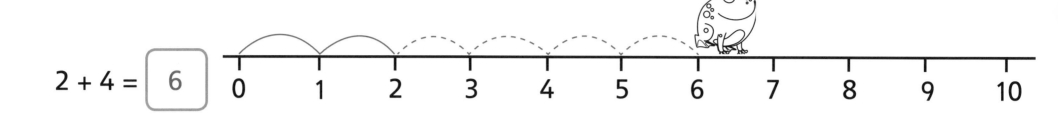

$2 + 4 =$ 6

0 1 2 3 4 5 6 7 8 9 10

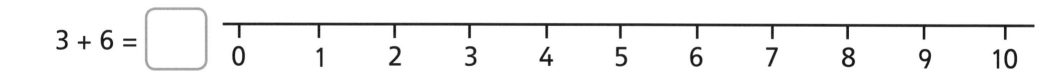

$5 + 2 =$

0 1 2 3 4 5 6 7 8 9 10

$3 + 6 =$

0 1 2 3 4 5 6 7 8 9 10

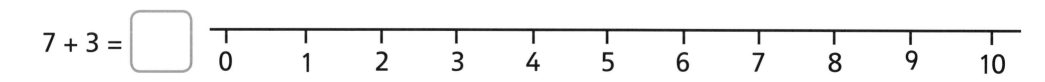

$7 + 3 =$

0 1 2 3 4 5 6 7 8 9 10

Key Language: *Add with a number line. (Two) plus (four) equals (six).* Point to each equation and read it aloud, e.g., *Two plus four equals* … Children count and draw the lines on the number line to arrive at the answer. Finally, children say the complete equation, e.g., *Two plus four equals six.* Optional: Children write the answer to complete the equation.

⬭ Trace. ○ Circle. ✖ Cross out.

turn on

turn off

recycle

plastic bag

cloth bag

trash

Key Language: *plastic bag, cloth bag, recycle, trash, turn on, turn off.* Children look at each picture and trace it as they repeat the word. Finally, children circle the pictures of items or actions that help the Earth and cross out the ones that don't. Optional: They trace the words as well.

109

✏️ Color. ✏️ Draw. 💬 Say.

Key Language: *What can you do to help the Earth? I can (recycle ... / use cloth bags / turn off the lights).* Children look at each picture. Then they draw themselves in the empty face. They choose one good action that can help the Earth. Finally, children present their pages and say, e.g., *I can recycle paper. I can turn off the lights.*

 **Look.** **Draw.** **Say.**

What do you think about...?

Key Language: *What do you think about ... (pollution)? I think (bees) are ... I think (pollution) is ... (beautiful / ugly / boring / interesting / terrible / great / bad / important).* Point to the character and ask: *What do you think about ...?* Then point to each picture and repeat: *What do you think about bees? ... pollution? ... frogs?* Children think and draw a happy, sad, scared or bored expression on the faces. Finally, repeat the question and invite children to give their opinions using the language, e.g., *I think (bees) are (important).*

👁 Look. ✏ Color. 💬 Say.

Key Language: *Can we recycle this? What's it made of? It's made of glass / plastic / paper.* Children look at the scene. Ask: *What's wrong?* (*There is trash in the ocean. / The ocean is polluted. / The fish are sad.*) Then ask: *What can we do to help?* (*We can take care of the ocean and the fish. We can recycle.*) Have children color all of the things that can be recycled. Finally, point to each object and ask: *Can we recycle this? What's it made of?* and guide children to answer: *Yes, we can recycle this. It's made of (plastic / glass / paper).*

2⅓ Count. ◯ Circle. ◌ Trace.

70 — 80 — 90

70 — 80 — 90

Key Language: *How many (flowers) can you see? Let's count by tens: ten, twenty, thirty, forty, fifty, sixty, seventy, eighty, ninety. Sets of ten. Nine sets of ten.* Children say the number: *ninety.* Then they look at the first frame. Ask: *How many flowers?* Guide children to notice that if they count down the first column it is a set of 10. Say: *Let's count by tens.* And count across the columns: *Ten, twenty, thirty, forty, fifty, sixty, seventy, eighty, ninety.* Children say and circle the correct number. Repeat with the soda cans. Optional: Children trace the number 90 with different colors.

 Say. ✏ Draw.

How can we care for the Earth?

Draw four new words you learned.

Draw a picture of your favorite part of the unit.

How did you do?

Key Language: *natural, human-made, frog, rock, paper, plastic bottle, cardboard box, soda can, newspaper, spoon, Is it natural or human-made? plastic bag, cloth bag, recycle, trash, turn on, turn off, What can you do to help the Earth? I can recycle newspaper. I can turn off the lights. I can save water.* Ask the Big Question: *How can we care for the Earth?* Children look back through the unit to recall what they have learned. Read the first two tasks together. Children draw their responses. Finally, guide children to read the last question and have them give themselves a "grade" by drawing a happy or a sad face.

9 What do we do on vacation?

🗨 **Say.** ✏ **Color.** ⭕ **Trace.**

beach

mountains

forest

amusement park

lake

summer camp

Key Language: *beach, mountains, forest, lake, amusement park, summer camp.* Ask the Big Question: *What do we do on vacation?* Children point to and name each place. Discuss which places children have visited and allow them to share experiences. Finally, children color the places they have been to on vacation. Optional: Children trace the words as they say them.

■ **Say.** ○ **Circle.** ✏ **Color.**

Percy's Peak

Key Language: *What can you see? Who are the characters? What are they doing? How do they feel? Where does the story take place? What's the story about? mountains, walk.* Children look at the story scenes. Ask the literacy questions. Then ask: *Can you see Charlie? Can you see Sharon? Can you see mom and dad walking? Can you see mountains?* Children circle and then color the items in the picture.

Say. ◯ Circle. ✏ Color.

Key Language: *What can you see? Who are the characters? What are they doing? How do they feel? Where does the story take place? What's the story about?* children, happy, sad, tired, shine. Children look at the story scenes. Ask the literacy questions. Then ask: *Can you see the children feeling sad and tired? Can you see the sun shining? Can you see the children feeling happy?* Children circle and then color the items in the picture. Then they retell the story in their own words. Provide language as needed.

 **Draw.** **Say.** **Color.**

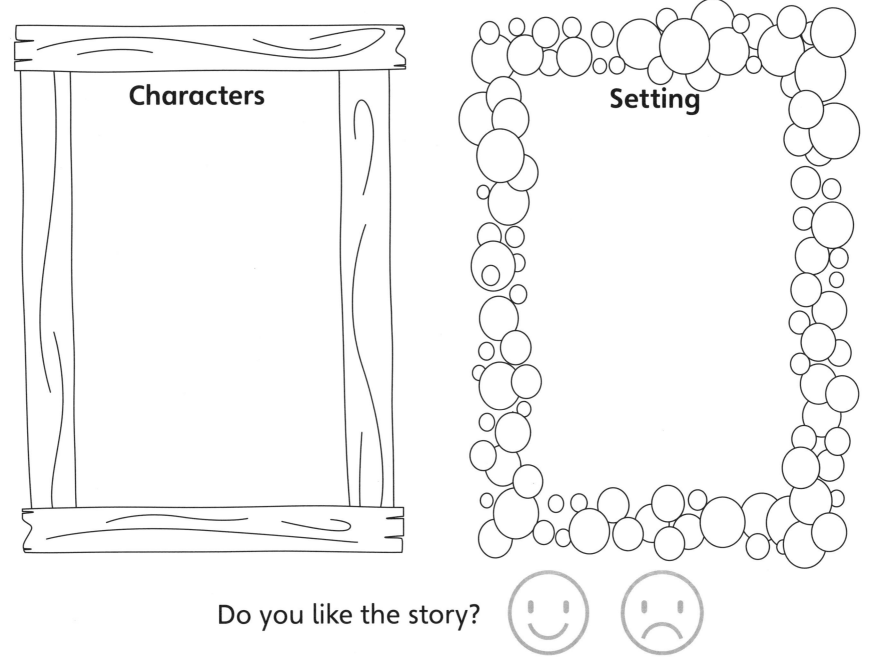

Characters

Setting

Do you like the story?

Key Language: *Can you remember? Who are the characters? Where does the story take place?* Ask the first two literacy questions and encourage all answers. Children can look back at the story if necessary. Children draw the characters (Charlie and Sharon, and their parents). Repeat with the second question and have children draw the mountains. Then they present their drawings using the language: *The characters are ... The story takes place in ...* Finally, ask: *Do you like the story? (Yes. / No.)* Children color the happy face or the sad face.

🔲 **Say.** ✘ **Cross out.** 🔲 **Talk.**

Key Language: *pick up our trash, don't litter, take care of nature.* Children look at the scene and say what they see. Ask: *Where are they? (On vacation. In the forest.)* Then ask: *What's wrong? (The family needs to pick up the trash.)* Children cross out the trash. Then they color in the scene. Finally, discuss why it's important to pick up our garbage when we're in nature.

🔲 Say. 🗨 Talk. ✎ Write.

cap			
towel			
sunglasses			

flashlight			
sleeping bag			
backpack			

Key Language: *towel, flashlight, sleeping bag, sunglasses, cap, backpack.* Point to and have children name each item in the first column. Demonstrate asking and answering about these items with a confident child. Ask: *Do you have a cap? Do you have a sleeping bag?* etc. Make a check mark or an X depending on their answer. Arrange children in pairs and have them ask each other and record their answers with check marks or Xs. Repeat with new partners. If the children are confident enough, they could write their classmates' names at the top of each column.

✏️ Draw. 💬 Say.

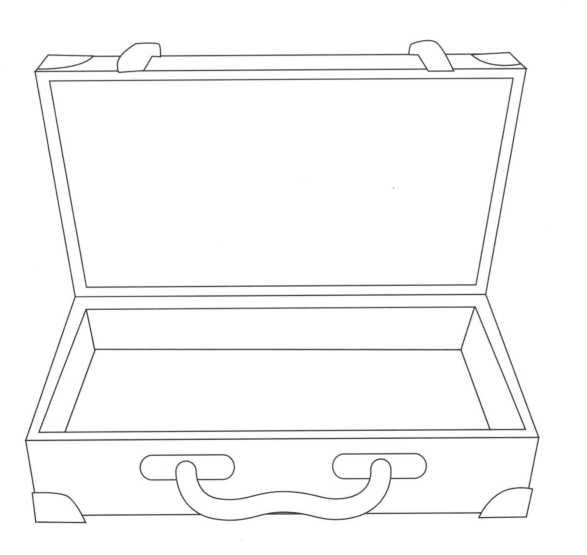

Key Language: *What do you take to the (beach)? I take a (towel) to the (beach).* Point to the top row of items and ask children to name them. Then bring their attention to the empty suitcase and ask: *Where do you want to go on vacation?* Children decide where to go on vacation. Then say: *What do you take to the (beach)? Please, draw!* Children draw what they want to take in their suitcase. Finally, they present their suitcases using the language, e.g., *I take sunglasses and a towel to the beach. I take a sleeping bag and backpack to summer camp.*

$2\frac{1}{3}$ Count. ✏ Draw. 🗨 Say.

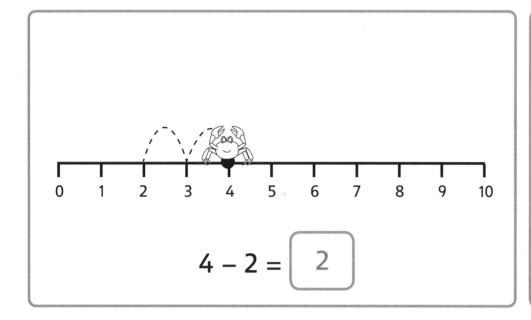

$$4 - 2 = \boxed{2}$$

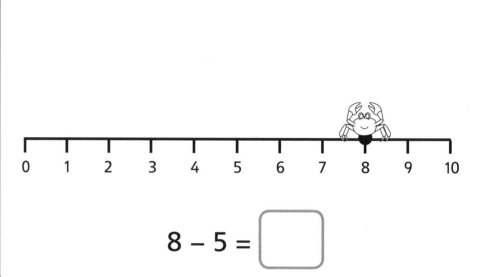

$$8 - 5 = \boxed{}$$

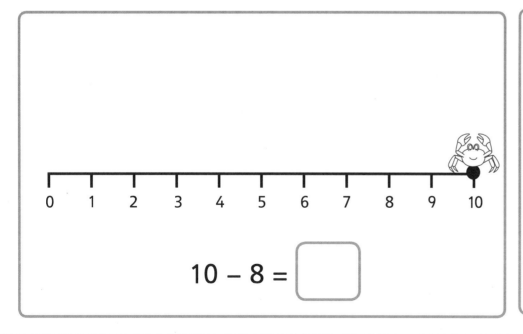

$$10 - 8 = \boxed{}$$

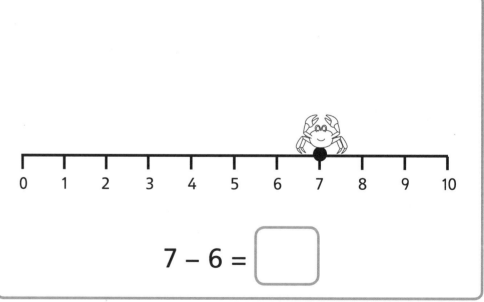

$$7 - 6 = \boxed{}$$

Key Language: Subtract with a number line. (Four) minus (two) equals (two). Point to each equation and read it aloud: *Four minus two equals* ... Then children count and draw the lines on the number line. Finally, children say the completed equation, e.g., *Four minus two equals two.* Optional: Children write the answers in the boxes.

🗨 Say. ◌ Trace.

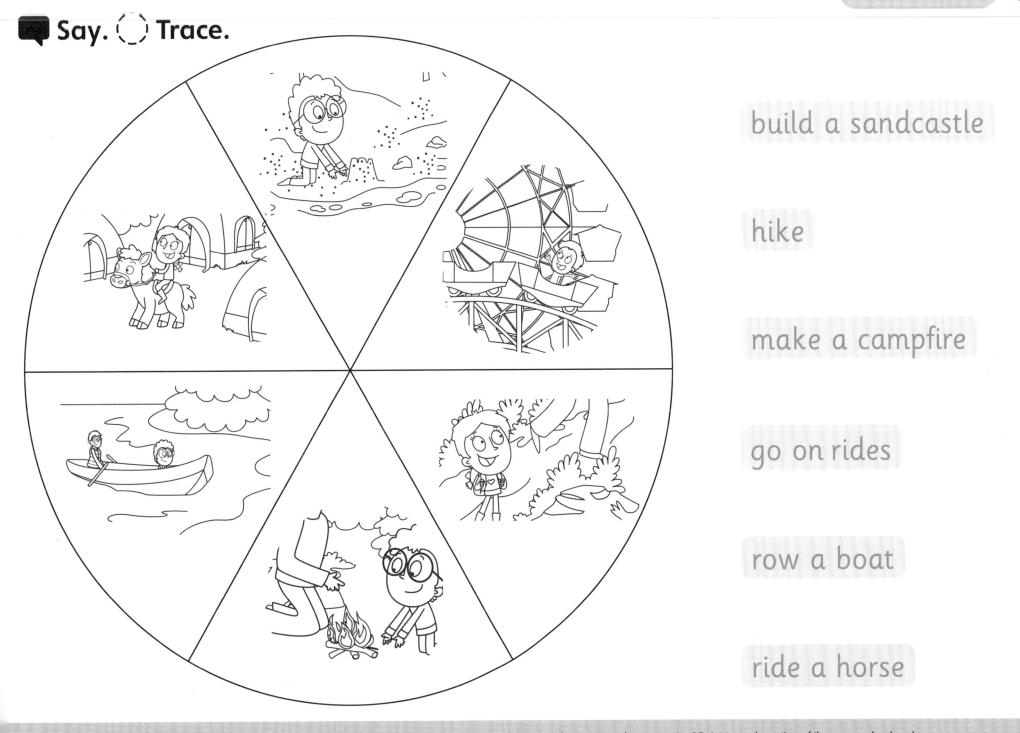

build a sandcastle

hike

make a campfire

go on rides

row a boat

ride a horse

Key Language: *build a sandcastle, hike, make a campfire, row a boat, ride a horse, go on rides.* Ask: *What can you do on vacation?* Point to each section of the game wheel and have children name the activities. Demonstrate how to play the game. Have a volunteer put a pen or pencil in the middle of the circle and spin it. Have everyone look at the picture the pencil is pointing to and repeat the question: *What can you do on vacation?* The child answers, e.g., *Make a campfire.* Arrange children in small groups and let them play, providing help as needed. Optional: Children trace the words.

👁 Look. ✏ Color. 💬 Say.

Key Language: *What does s/he do (in the mountains / at the beach)? S/he (hikes / builds a sandcastle).* Children look at the pictures. Ask: *What does Mia do at the beach?* Children color the pictures that show activities Mia does at the beach. Finally, children take turns describing activities, saying e.g., *Mia builds a sandcastle at the beach.*

 Look. Draw. Say.

Key Language: *Where are you going on vacation? I'm going to the ... What are you going to do? I'm going to ...* Point to the first person and read their question aloud: *Where are you going on vacation?* Then look at the pictures of Mia and Leo's vacation plans and read together. Then children think about where they are going on vacation or where they want to go and draw a picture. Ask volunteers to share their drawings with the class and describe them, e.g., *I'm going to the beach. I'm going to build a sandcastle. I'm going to take sunglasses.*

125

✏ Paint. 💬 Say.

Key Language: *What can you do at the beach? I can build a sandcastle.* Ask children: *What can you do at the beach?* and elicit: *Build a sandcastle!* Tell children to imagine their sandcastle. Distribute watercolors. Demonstrate painting the beach with yellow or brown across the page and then paint the sandcastle. Go around to each painting and sprinkle some sand (salt) on the paintings while they are still wet. When the salt dries, the effect will look fantastic. Have children present their sandcastles, saying: *I can build a sandcastle!*

➡️➡️ Follow. 2¹₃ Count. ⭕ Trace.

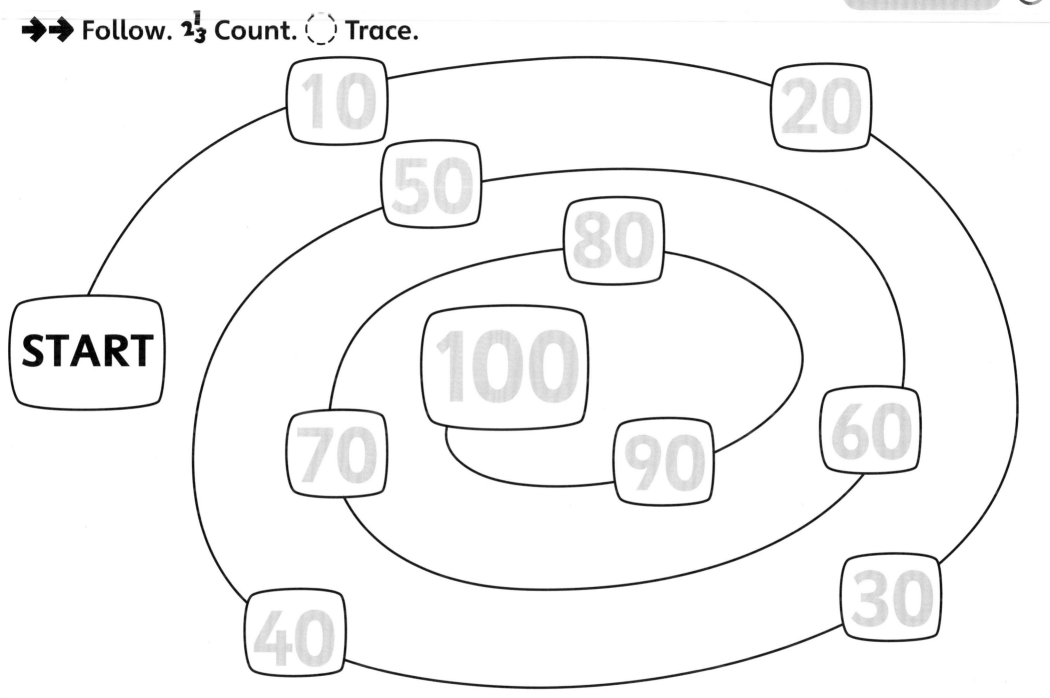

Key Language: *Let's count by tens: ten, twenty, thirty, forty, fifty, sixty, seventy, eighty, ninety, one hundred.* Children follow the path and count by tens as they go. When they reach one hundred, they trace the number lots of times with different colored crayons, repeating: *One hundred!* Optional: Children trace the numbers while they repeat the words.

127

 Say. ✏ Draw.

What do we do on vacation?

Draw four new words you learned.

Draw a picture of your favorite part of the unit.

How did you do?

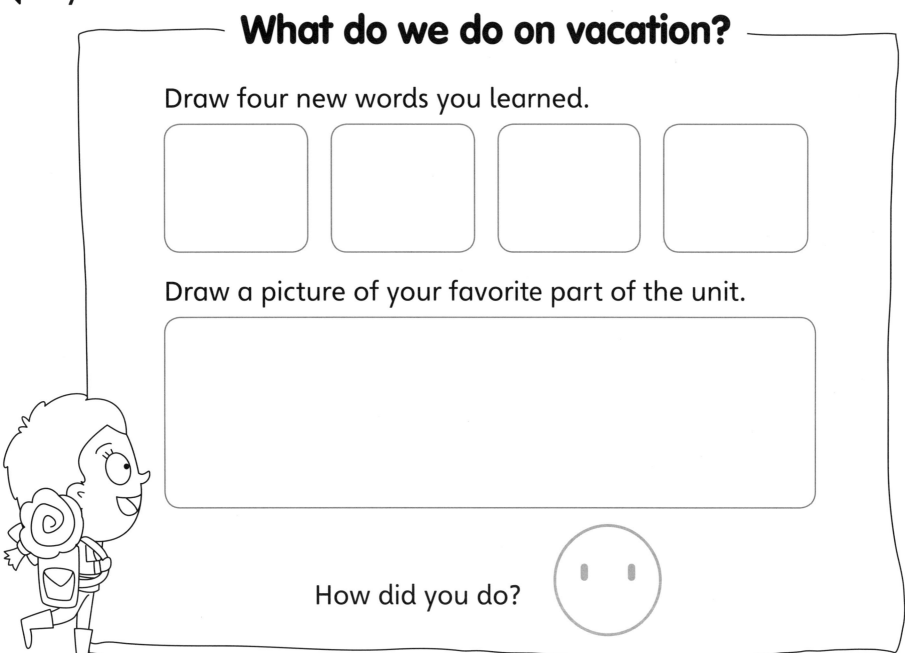

Key Language: *beach, mountains, forest, amusement park, lake, summer camp, cap, towel, sunglasses, sleeping bag, backpack, flashlight, What do you take to the (beach)? I take a (towel) to the beach), build a sandcastle, hike, make a campfire, go on rides, row a boat, ride a horse. What do you do (in the mountains)? I (hike).* Ask the Big Question: *What do we do on vacation?* Children look back through the unit to recall what they have learned. Read the first two tasks together. Children draw their responses. Finally, guide children to read the last question and have them give themselves a "grade" by drawing a happy or a sad face.

Picture Dictionary

Children open the book to the corresponding unit. Then they point to a picture and name it. If children cannot name the vocabulary item, say the word and have them repeat it. Finally, children color the pictures.

129

Unit 1 / Vocabulary 1	Unit 1 / Vocabulary 2	Unit 1 / Vocabulary 3	Unit 2 / Vocabulary 1

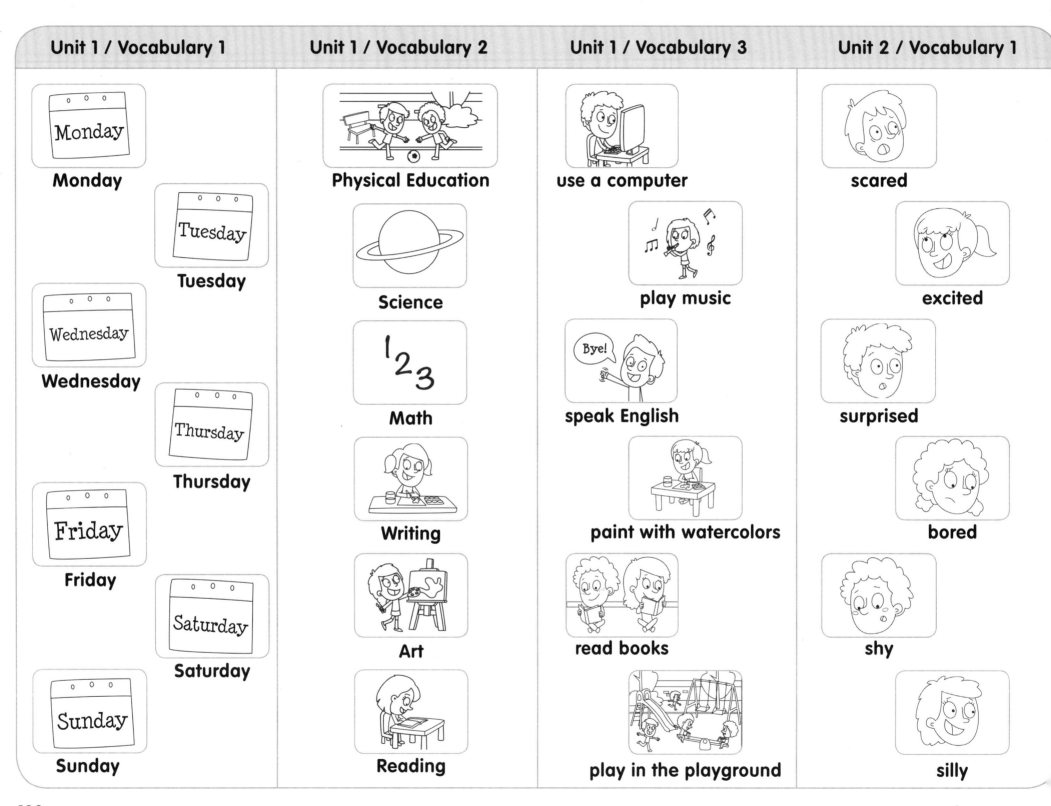

Unit 1 / Vocabulary 1

Monday

Tuesday

Wednesday

Thursday

Friday

Saturday

Sunday

Unit 1 / Vocabulary 2

Physical Education

Science

Math

Writing

Art

Reading

Unit 1 / Vocabulary 3

use a computer

play music

speak English

paint with watercolors

read books

play in the playground

Unit 2 / Vocabulary 1

scared

excited

surprised

bored

shy

silly

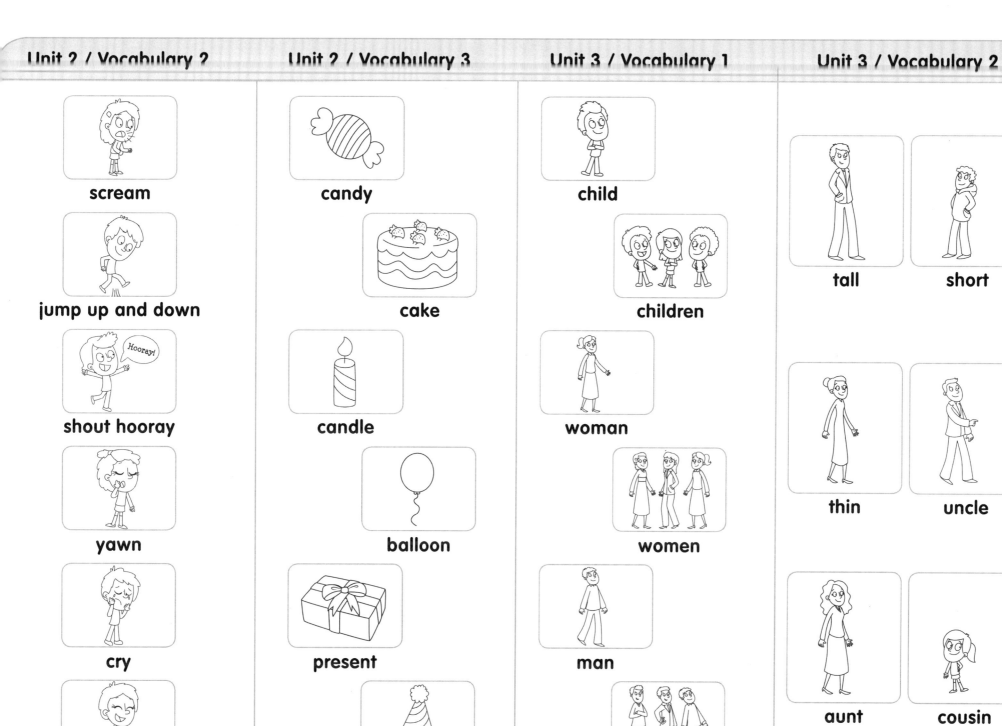

Unit 2 / Vocabulary 2

scream

jump up and down

shout hooray

yawn

cry

laugh

Unit 2 / Vocabulary 3

candy

cake

candle

balloon

present

party hat

Unit 3 / Vocabulary 1

child

children

woman

women

man

men

Unit 3 / Vocabulary 2

tall

short

thin

uncle

aunt

cousin

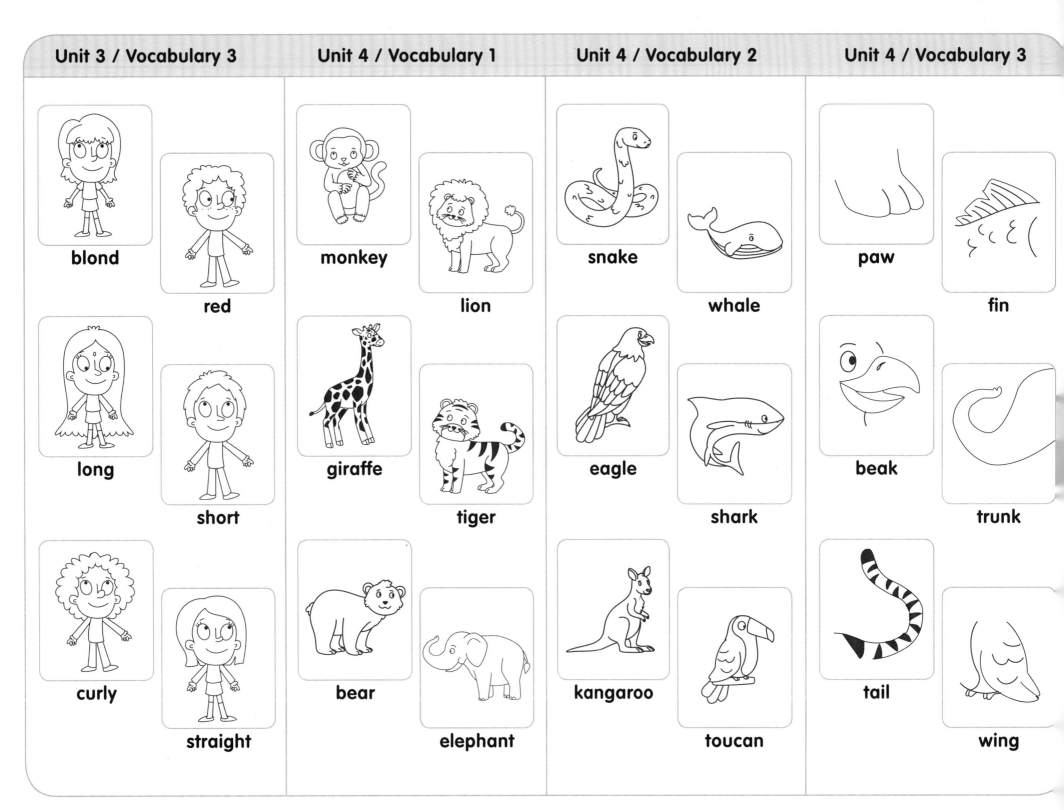

blond

red

long

short

curly

straight

monkey

lion

giraffe

tiger

bear

elephant

snake

whale

eagle

shark

kangaroo

toucan

paw

fin

beak

trunk

tail

wing

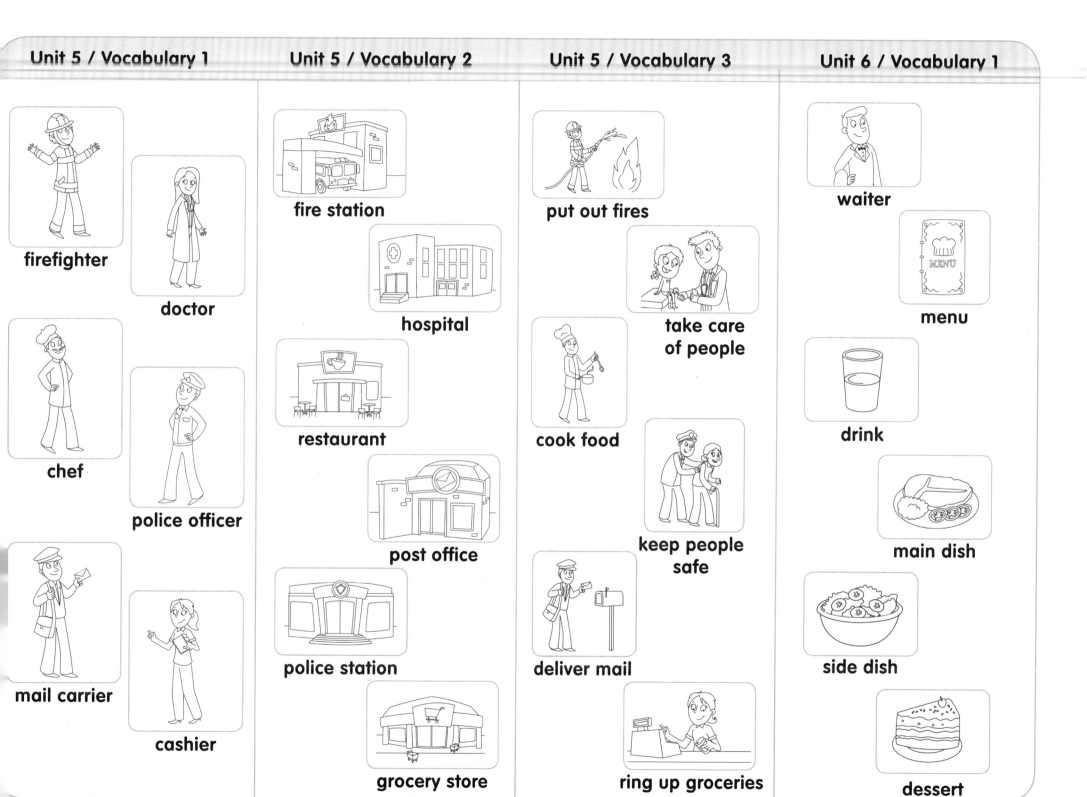

firefighter

doctor

chef

police officer

mail carrier

cashier

fire station

hospital

restaurant

post office

police station

grocery store

put out fires

take care of people

cook food

keep people safe

deliver mail

ring up groceries

waiter

menu

drink

main dish

side dish

dessert

Unit 6 / Vocabulary 2	Unit 6 / Vocabulary 3	Unit 7 / Vocabulary 1	Unit 7 / Vocabulary 2
lemonade	 spaghetti	 get up	dance class
soda	 pizza	 get dressed	 soccer practice
steak	 ice cream	have breakfast	music lessons
 rice	 chocolate cake	 go to school	swimming lessons
 beans	 steamed vegetables	go home	play with friends
 French fries	 cheeseburger	do homework	 gymnastics

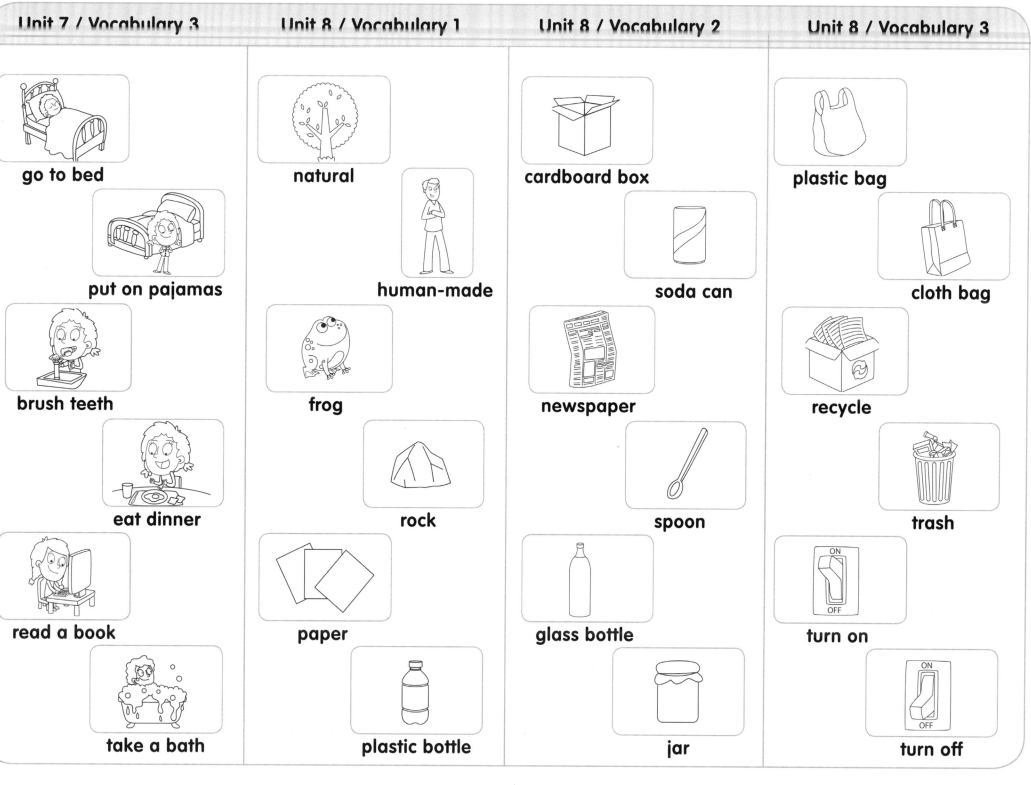

Unit 7 / Vocabulary 3

go to bed

put on pajamas

brush teeth

eat dinner

read a book

take a bath

Unit 8 / Vocabulary 1

natural

human-made

frog

rock

paper

plastic bottle

Unit 8 / Vocabulary 2

cardboard box

soda can

newspaper

spoon

glass bottle

jar

Unit 8 / Vocabulary 3

plastic bag

cloth bag

recycle

trash

turn on

turn off

beach

mountains

forest

amusement park

lake

summer camp

towel

flashlight

sleeping bag

sunglasses

cap

backpack

build a sandcastle

hike

make a campfire

go on rides

row a boat

ride a horse